MARIO CAMPI · FRANCO PESSINA
Architects

Essays by Werner Seligmann and Jorge Silvetti
Photographed and compiled by Eduard Hueber
Series Editor, Kenneth Frampton

RIZZOLI
NEW YORK

Published in the United States of America
in 1987 by RIZZOLI INTERNATIONAL PUBLICATIONS,
INC.
597 Fifth Avenue
New York, N.Y. 10017

Design by Silvia Kolbowski
Typography by Strong Silent Type
Printed and bound in Hong Kong

LC 86-43206

ISBN 0-8478-0799-1

*Cover: Gymnasium, Neggio,
Switzerland, 1980. Entrance facade
detail.*

MARIO CAMPI · FRANCO PESSINA
Architects

CONTENTS

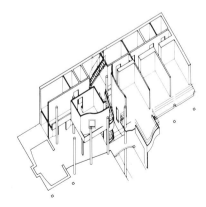

THE WORK OF CAMPI · PESSINA: AN INTRODUCTION

Jorge Silvetti

For some time now there has been significant international interest in the architecture of the Ticino canton in Switzerland. Yet, up until the present the work of the Ticinese firm, Campi·Pessina, has been known in America mainly in academic circles, and there only through the accounts of a few connoisseurs, or through the lectures of its most traveled member, Mario Campi. The Campi·Pessina office in Lugano has been a mecca to an initiated group of American students that have visited and worked there and then passed the secret on to others. It is not because it is obscure, arcane, or exotic in form and content that the remarkable work of this firm is not more widely known. Nor is it because the work is geographically too remote or inaccessible. Campi·Pessina have, in fact, produced a body of buildings and projects that stem from commissions from both the private and public sectors, that accommodate conventional programs (schools, gymnasia, banks, single family houses, housing, commercial interiors, etc.) and that accept, display and elaborate the conventional elements of architecture. The work can be found in its entirety in the most accessible area of the Italian-speaking sector of Switzerland, in the vicinity of the firm's office near Lake Lugano. That the work of Campi·Pessina, which spans more than twenty years of continuous productivity, is being presented here precisely at this moment is, in my view, the result of a particular *shift* that is occurring in architectural sensibilities from the facile polemics that have recently dominated the architectural press and education in America to more sober and mature preoccupations, perceptions, and expectations.

However adventurous and even difficult it may seem to attempt to understand that shift and the evolving sensibilities of our times as they occur and involve us, it is an essential effort to undertake in an introduction of this work to an American audience, lest this book pass on as just another catalog of beautifully printed architectural images.

Both partners of the firm, Mario Campi and Franco Pessina, belong to the generation of architects that received its education during the late part of the 1950s, which is to say during the time when enough of modern architecture had been built and tested to have comprised a body of knowledge, but when a critical and historical consciousness had not yet developed, even though the seeds for this consciousness had already been planted. To those conditions may be added the particularly narrow adherence to modernist principles practiced in Switzerland in those years, probably due to its peculiar status as a neutral country during the then recently ended war. This status fostered a certain "amnesia" regarding the ideological and social programs of modern architecture, programs which were renewed in the rest of Europe by the post-war reconstruction of its cities. In place of these programs, and aided by the economic stability of the country, creative and polemical energies were channeled into perfecting an architecture that was impeccably detailed and executed, and that faithfully developed the most "objective" aspects of architecture.

As Mario Campi said about the ETH (Eidgenossische Technische Hochschule) in Zurich (the outstanding Swiss school of architecture in those years and the one from which he obtained his professional degree), it was a school where ". . . history was not considered to be too important, and was taught mostly as a stylistic matter," and where ". . . most of the teaching focused almost exclusively on the technological and functional aspects of architecture." In these areas the school in particular and the Swiss in general excelled, and this strength may still be responsible, together with resources, stability, and traditions, for the overall high quality of building in Switzerland. The predominance of this amnesiac yet intense faith in modern architecture, practiced and sanctioned by the German-Swiss, did not provide a base for the development of theory and criticism as we understand it today, and the lack of polemics—which to a degree still characterized the ETH until recently—had its roots in these conditions.

But differing from the mainstream of Swiss architecture, as in so many other aspects of their culture, the "marginal" Ticinese, among them Campi and Pessina (and Niki Piazzoli, who left the firm in 1984, sought a balance to what already seemed to them a rather restrictive architectural scene. They looked to nearby Milan, where Ernesto Nathan Rogers was beginning to lay new foundations of architectural theory and criticism in post-war Europe, with a focus that was "continuous" with the modern tradition, not paralyzed by dogma, and enriched with a positive view of history. For those like Campi and Pessina who had been "trained" to practice the modern art of good building, who then were touched by the architectural thinking and practices of the critical minds of Milan, a subtle, serious and very particular set of values was established and an orientation that has no equivalent in contemporary architectural culture.

This set of values brought together in an unlikely marriage an untroubled faith in the building as a result of program, technology, and an ensuing rigorous execution, with the sobering realization that the city was not the result of a Project, but a construction of Time and Culture. This matching would tend, one imagines today, to defuse the antihistorical polemics of Modernism without renouncing its most valuable technological and figurative contributions. It would, in a subtle, almost sweet way historicize modernity and dispel as irrelevant, for architecture at least, the abstraction versus representation argument. In the broader picture, other currents were added to the powerful new criticism in Italy, particularly in England during the same period, which reflected tendencies that were more inclusive, iconographic, and populist, and that would be sensed more profoundly in America.

It was in this context of incipient but irreversible theoreti-

cal change that the firm settled in Lugano in 1962 and began to work. It is this context too which may shed some light on what Campi was demanding of architects a few years ago at Harvard's Graduate School of Design when he stated that "it is over the years that one comes to understand that what counts is the *honesty* and *thoroughness* of the work." It is probably the consistency with which their production has been honest with respect to social and cultural demands, and their practice thorough in regard to professional obligations, that has placed them and their work in a somewhat awkward position with respect to the parallel developments in architectural theory, criticism, and practice in America during these same decades.

For while certain important foundations of architectural theory and criticism in continental Europe had been laid out from *within* the discipline itself, in the United States the impetus was given by the eruption of critical tendencies of a more general pedigree and application, such as the new directions in literary criticism, and the ambitious projects of semiotics and post-structuralism. In light of these approaches, we began to look at Architecture with a more exhaustive, inclusive lens, as a fact of culture, as a system of signs, as a text to be read. All of this allowed us to distance ourselves from the already stifling canons and mindless personal "expressionisms" that characterized so much of the architecture of the 1960's. The general theories of language and culture afforded a richer and more comprehensive view of the possibilities and obligations of Architecture, and the ideas of "convention" and "discipline" re-emerged as moving forces in the formulation of a new program for an architecture that was "post-modern." Together with language, discipline, and convention and as a consequence of them, an involvement with history was reinstated as a necessary foundation of the theory and practice of architecture.

The work of Campi·Pessina presents a balanced and convincing case for these reformulated foundations. In the 1970s, Campi sought in America, as he had done in the 1960s in Milan, contact with these new sources of thought and ideas. He began in the late 1970s to teach almost regularly at Syracuse, Cornell, and Harvard Universities, and at the Rhode Island School of Design. Thus the firm was not unaware of the development of American Post-Modernism, and some of the figural shifts in Campi·Pessina's production, notably evident in the Arosio House of 1980 and the Polloni House of 1981, reflect a conscious break with previous vocabulary and the opening of new lines of research.

And yet this work was not taken up to illustrate, indeed does not serve well to illustrate, the concerns of the American version of Post-Modernism through the 1970s. For, a closer look at American Post-Modernism reveals that other interests and forces were operating (or, more accurately, other modes, as I do not believe they were conscious) which would not allow this architecture to participate in the parade of new portents.

The dominant stream of Post-Modernism in the 1970s in the United States was, in general, not a constructive, positive critique that allowed architects to build upon modern architecture's best contributions. Rather, it was a proclaimed rupture and denial of what had preceded, and the establishment of supposedly "new grounds" (or the re-establishment of "eternal" ones, depending on the particular rhetorical strategy). And while the critique had sound foundations, the "solution" existed purely at the level of image and vocabulary. Because what for many still passes as a "recovery" of History, as a return to tradition and convention in architecture, was neither more nor less than a replay of one of the most debilitating forces of late twentieth century art as reflected in Architecture. That is, the idea of constant change contained in modernist avantgarde strategies which sponsored the search for continuous innovation, novelty, and originality, a process interpreted not as a perfecting of but as a break with what preceded, as opposition and as rebellion. This was the tired condition of architecture in this period which paradoxically closed the circle of references, seemingly exhausted the modernist vocabulary, and posited the only possible response as that of a return to History: a rhetorical and ideological necessity to comply with that self-destructive energy that in Architecture resolved its polemical urge in purely iconographic terms.

The work of Campi·Pessina did not score well in this type of game, despite its apparent coincidence with some of the underlying principles. Their steady, constant, thorough involvement with their own "oeuvre" has generated a body of work that is concerned with its own clarification at each new move, on each new building, that honestly poses at each step a self-critique of what has preceded and builds upon it rather than shifting directions to attempt novel images. This course of action, besides its inherent challenges and the time needed to "construct" its case, is not the strategy of consumption and fashion. This is particularly so because the make-up of their own theoretical basis never includes "representation" as a polemical issue or aesthetic choice, but sees it as the way in which *all architecture* signifies. Consequently, Campi·Pessina were not competing in the war of images that dominated American architecture during the last ten years.

And although that contest did generate lively debates and heady moments, together with revelations and outrage, we know now that it was performed at the expense of a clarification of the artistic content of architecture. The images, operations, and arguments that were produced suffered the fate that all late avant-garde works had: they were quickly consumed, and the seemingly "creative" revival of Style is about to overwhelm if not obliterate our field of reference.

In addition to this iconographic impulse in Post-Modernism and the complexities in the areas of theory and criticism, another direction developed stemming from those initial incursions into the Language of Architecture. For, while one inevitable direction of research in Language leads into a purely iconographic, stylistic *dead end*, another inexorable path of research into language concludes with a critique of its own metaphysical foundations. This phenomenon corresponds precisely to the arrival and consumption of Post-Structuralism that marked these past few years of Post-Modernism. This powerful, effervescent, and short-lived chapter gave us the most daring insights into ideology, the unconscious, and the limits of Form and Representation, but also placed us at the edge of the Nietzschean abyss, which when considered as a critical force contributing to the development of Architecture as a discipline, begins to look misplaced if not spurious. This other direction of Post-Modernism reformulated and recreated a whole field of criticism, but it also *distanced* itself from any possible relationship with purpose, materiality, and practice. Campi·Pessina had no interest in establishing connections to this position.

Between these marginal strategies of Post-Modernism, "the dead end" of iconography and the "distancing" of metaphysics, there is an "emptiness" in the center. But this center, non-polemical by comparison and placement, is empty only in that it is defined by that which these two polarities are not. It is concerned with building execution, technological accuracy, functional sophistication and with seemingly bypassed issues such as lighting and luminosity. It is work that sees History as neither the repository of images nor as Myth to be destroyed, but rather as source of knowledge and continuity. It is work that ignores mimicry and self-effacing strategies and assumes the risks of building buildings that possess their own integrity in concrete sites. It is to these defining traits of a "non-polemical" center, that the work of Campi·Pessina seems to adjust more accurately. So it is not surprising that, as Post-Modernism shows signs of exhaustion and no

one but the confused are tempted to revive an iconographically naive Modernism, work such as that of Campi·Pessina, which previously occupied the silent space of "non-polemics," begins to distinguish itself.

But then, what are we to think about an architecture of non-polemics, of an architecture that interests us because of its qualities and yet appears to generate no words? Can we conceive today of a contemporary architecture that does not fall within the well-established dualisms of current polemics: classic *versus* modern, modern *versus* postmodern, representational *versus* abstraction?

I would argue that the questions raised by the polemics of Post-Modern architecture will never allow us to assess such architectures as that of Campi·Pessina. Their work is much more than just the filling of a void in the center. It is not that their work is non-polemic, or that it does not generate words, but rather, that American Post-Modernism has given us no words and no framework within which to discuss it, or, to borrow an idiom from contemporary theory, it contains a polemics, the "polemicity" of which has been forgotten by most critics.

It is through the ever more visible cracks of the existing debate that we begin to intuit the value of Campi·Pessina's work. This act of discernment is an effect of the shift in sensibilities, perceptions and preoccupations that I referred to at the beginning of this text; we are beginning to be able to see differently, and yet we are not yet able to speak.

Furthermore, through the close examination of the work of Campi·Pessina, not as individual work but as representative of a tendency, we are able to question the seemingly "objective" categorizations that have defined the architecture of the Ticino region to date. For, at the risk of complicating matters, but necessarily in order to further a clearer understanding of this work, we should also refer to another move made by contemporary criticism that seemingly includes this work, but which does so by diminishing its stature.

In the last decade what has caught the attention of some critics, architects and historians is the "discovery" of an architecture of the Ticino region, which some have even labeled the "School of Ticino," and to which the work of Campi·Pessina would surely belong. This discovery by now has been discussed and presented many times. The reasons for both this "discovery" and the interest it has generated are convincing and compelling: the long, continuous tradition of great architect-builders from the Ticino, that begins in the 16th century with Domenico Fontana, Carlo Maderno, and Francesco Borromini; the fact of the Ticino being a well-defined geographical and cultural region within a country and, in particular, the eagerness of architects and critics to find built architectural evidence of the Italian counterproposal to American Post-Modernism, that is, neo-Rationalism, that was nowhere to be found in reasonable abundance in Italy itself, but that existed in the Italian part of Switzerland. Finally, on the part of the Ticinese themselves, a corresponding eagerness for a cultural identity different from that of the rest of the country. This attitude precipitated a search for identifying characteristics common to the architecture of the region, and consequently encouraged the production of conceptual categories that fit so neatly into a critical framework. On closer look, however, most of the arguments concerning the architecture of the Ticino are little more than a series of catchwords produced by the Modernism vs. Post-Modernism polemics as they do not address the truly rich tradition and dense reality of the architecture of the region, and serve mainly as a way to present the architecture of a single protagonist: Mario Botta. Indeed, for all of Botta's general value, most critics have presented his work as an illustration of a resistance to both the iconographic and the nihilistic tendencies of Post-Modernism, and in so doing proclaimed it to be the logical inheritor of modernity. That Botta's pedigree was complex, different from other Ticino architects in that it included Louis Kahn and Rossi, so as to disclaim an easy and direct connection with modernity, was not so important as the fact that the images were *abstract*. Paradoxically, the case for Botta's status as inheritor of the modernist legacy was built around this issue.

And, of course, this diminished reading of Botta's work did present a polemic, did generate words, by fitting into the oppositional rubrics, such as "representation" versus "abstraction" that were so much in vogue in the early 1980s. Most importantly, the images were compelling, alluring, apparently novel and, in the end, photogenically consumable. But because the "School of Ticino" was illustrated with such a particular and extreme case, and this reduced to the level of pure and powerful images, work such as that of Campi·Pessina and some other Ticinese was not seen in a more comprehensive and subtle light. And of all the contemporary controversies that bore so little relevance to their work, the polarization of representation versus abstraction has the least validity for the ideology and practice of Campi·Pessina. For them, architecture always *represents* something, and it always represents *through a process of abstraction*.

I have talked, so far, in the negative: about why and how the work of Campi·Pessina has not been recognized properly, and I am aware of the discomfort this may produce in the reader. I could have concentrated just on the images that this book contains, powerful and positive images, and analyzed them critically with attention to their pedigree and their status in contemporary architecture. But to do this in an introduction of this work would have been to orient the reading of their work in the manner of iconographic Post-Modernism, which would inevitably emphasize the visual seductiveness of the photographs and lead to their quick consumption. More importantly, in allowing this uncritical reading I would have lost the opportunity that their work and its history offers us, very persuasively, to reorient and recharge an argument and a productive polemic about current conditions for the practice of architecture. This negative stance was then an intentional rhetorical ploy undertaken in an attempt to point to some of the failings of contemporary criticism that require immediate revision, if theory is to aid practice as I believe it should.

I am convinced that, as the critical apparatus formulated by some Post-Modernist approaches, based on the unproductive oppositions and self-destructive strategies of the avant-garde, continues to lose strength, we will find exemplary and provocative works for which we have had hitherto no conceptual categories, and of which we had been unable to speak. It seems that any program for reinvigorating and redirecting architectural theory and criticism will have to start not solely from the revision of philosophical foundations and the establishment of relationships with other domains of knowledge, but also and necessarily from a critical involvement with the act of building, with materiality, and execution. This will help us to reposition architecture in the field of social practices, particularly with respect to Power in general and to Art in particular, two institutions with which it has had a most equivocal relationship during this period of Post-Modernism.

Work like that of Campi·Pessina requires looking at architecture with very different lenses than the ones we have been using, lenses that "deform" architecture in slightly different ways and focus on features that Post-Modernism has tended to overlook, investigating its materiality in place of seeing through it. Because of this, their work returns to us, in a very convincing and novel way, issues about building, materials, detailing and execution. And it does this without overlooking image and iconography but also without using them polemically. Instead it makes at least two good cases. It makes a case for grounding archi-

tectural ideas in the inherent qualities of the discipline, rather than in other more general concerns. This then logically makes for another case for continuity (however difficult to comprehend this may be to the seekers of new images), with a past that now seems richer and more generous as it includes, in a contradictory but not tragic sense, the good lessons of Modernity. In making these cases, this work will necessarily be subjected to critical assessment, but then it will be done on more productive critical grounds.

THE POETICS OF COUNTERPOINT

Werner Seligmann

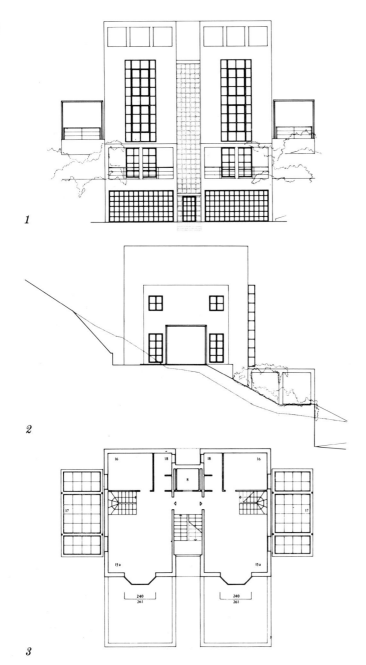

1

2

3

In the 1960s, the creative center of Swiss architecture shifted from the German-speaking cantons to the Ticino, the canton south of the Alps that border Italy. The northern part of Switzerland has played a significant role in the evolution of modern architecture, although to this day the work of architects such as Paul Ataria and Hans Schmidt, Werner Moser, Max Haefli and Rudolf Steiger, Hans Brechbuehler, Otto Senn, and Emil Roth is still relatively unknown outside of Switzerland. The best-known architecture from post-World War II Switzerland has been buildings and projects by Atelier 5 and the somewhat idiosyncratic work of Ernst Gisel, both representative of the northern cantons. In 1975, however, an exhibition of Ticinese architects was organized by the Eidgenossische Technishe Hochschule in Zurich, titled "Tendenzen: Neuere Architektur aus dem Tessin," and it came as a revelation to an architectural community unprepared for the extent and consistent quality of work that had been produced by a group of extraordinarily talented, almost unknown, young architects. A common approach was evident in the projects, and the title of the exhibition quickly provided a collective identity for the group and their work—"La Tendenza." The name was not without an implied reference to the "Rationalists" and "Gruppo 7."

Most of the "Tendenza" architects had originally been educated at the ETH. The ETH has long had an unofficial policy of having on its faculty at least one professor from the Italian-and one from the French-speaking cantons of Switzerland. In the post-World War II years, two professors, Rino Tami and Alberto Camenzind, were highly respected representatives of the Ticino at the ETH. An ultimately more influential presence, however, was that of Dolf Schnebli. Schnebli was from the German-speaking part of Switzerland and had been trained at both the ETH and Harvard University. In 1959, when he was faculty assistant to Moser, one of the pioneers of modern architecture in Switzerland, he won a competition for a school in Locarno and subsequently established a practice in Agno in the Ticino. He converted part of an old monastary overlooking Lake Lugano into an atelier that became a spiritual, intellectual, and educational hub for young architects from many countries. The quality of his work and the stimulation generated by his studio provided a model for the young Ticinese architects.

The most important influences, however, lay not to the north but to the south, with the presence, in neighboring Milan, of Aldo Rossi and the emerging neo-Rationalism. Geographically, if not geopolitically, the Ticino belongs to Italy north of the Po River. It is difficult to distinguish the landscape around Lugano from the sites of Lake Como or Lake Garda. It is an exceptionally romantic landscape, extending from the snowcapped Alps to the flat expanses of the Po valley. While the architects of this region declare themselves Swiss, their stronger spiritual, intellectual, and architectural ties are to Italy. They take pride in an architectural heritage that includes, they point out, three of the most significant architects of the Italian Baroque, all born in the region of Lugano: Domenico Fontana, Carlo Maderno, and Francesco Borromini. Furthermore, traditionally, a cultural axis runs from Lugano to Como and Milan, the birthplace of the Italian Rationalist movement in 1926, inaugurated by the work of Giuseppi Terragani and Pietro Lingeri. Despite their strong identification with Italy, however, the fact that the young Ticinese architects have built in Switzerland distinguishes them noticeably from their Italian neighbors. Because of its social stability and the density of its population, Switzerland has always maintained an extraordinarily high quality of construction and a sense of permanence in building. The training at the ETH instilled in the architects a very strong sense of craft and functionality.

Mario Campi not only studied in Zurich and produced his diploma project there under the guidance of Alfred Roth, one of the significant Swiss architects in the halcyon days of the Modern Movement, but also taught there in 1970 as an assistant to Schnebli. At about the same time, he opened an office in Lugano, together with two other young Ticinese architects, Niki Piazzoli and Franco Pessina. (Piazzoli was to leave the practice in 1984, for a new position as the Director of Federal Buildings for the Ticino.) In 1975 Campi assumed a teaching position in design at his alma mater. The extraordinary quality of the work of his studio resulted in 1977 in an offer to spend a semester at Syracuse University as a visiting critic. This was followed by invitations from Cornell University and the Graduate School of Design at Harvard University. Since that time, Campi has repeatedly taught and lectured in the United States. He has maintained the closest personal contact of any of the young Ticinese architects with his American contemporaries. There is no doubt that this has been a most fruitful exchange.

The early work of the firm is extremely inventive, but it was not until the mid-1970s, after Campi's first stay in the United States and after the neo-Rationalists had gained international recognition, that the work assumed a distinctly personal direction. The neo-Rationalist influences are the result of an almost filial respect and admiration on the part of Campi for Rossi. Campi·Pessina (and Campi·Pessina·Piazzoli) buildings have an obvious, immediate, and strong visual appeal that arises from the simplicity of their form, their easily recognizable ideas, and their exquisite details and careful construction. they are not, however, "one-liners". On careful examination, the buildings reveal extremely dense compositional invention and artistic rigor, and on these terms they require the serious involvement of the viewer. It is this quality that makes them architect's architects.

The Felder house of 1979 is the first project characteristic of their later work. The serene, Platonic, beautifully proportioned villa is located on the slope of a hill covered with vineyards, with beautiful views of the Alps to the east and of Lake Lugano to the south. A large, turn-of-the-century villa occupies the western section of the site. What distinguishes the solution is the way in which the architectural, typological characteristics of the existing building are ac-

11

12 cepted, and reinterpreted, thus creating a purer version of the same type. The new house, comparable in volume, shares an identical orientation and is placed as a complement directly adjacent to the existing building. The U-shaped parti of both buildings focus on the mountains. But the more recent structure is clearly an archetypal courtyard house, and the reference to historical models is unmistakable. True to the organizational model of the central courtyard house the circulation surrounds the courtyard, and, like its ancestor, the principal rooms of the house are directed inward and focus on the courtyard. The parti of the central courtyard house has been transposed by modifying and opening up one of its sides thereby establishing a preferred orientation. Nevertheless, the historical model remains legible and unmistakable due to the references expressed through the articulation of the enclosing walls, the fenestration, and the paved square. The transformation of the central courtyard to a U-shaped solution is not allowed to erode the purity of the house's volume. The space is registered on the exterior by four tall openings over the width of the courtyard. The resultant screen-wall acts as both the foreground to a view of the mountains and a space-defining device. The vertical members between the openings can be read as both colonnade and wall. The screen-wall can also be interpreted as a displaced courtyard wall minus its windows. The space between the square courtyard volume and the one defined to the south by the screen wall is planted with three trees, each in line with one of the vertical members of the wall. These trees can be viewed as foreground planting, but also as a minor order of columns, or as a substitute for the scale elements provided, in the archetypal courtyard house, by the fenestration.

The Polloni house of 1981 may be seen as a transformation of the Felder house achieved by turning the arms of the U to align with the main body of the house. The attitude expressed by the two buildings is similar, and the later represents only a further transformation of a type. The area belonging to the screen wall of the Felder house has been converted into a deep wall entrance zone at the street. The courtyard space has become a lateral zone between the house proper and the gate house. Although at first glance the elevations of the Felder house and the Polloni house appear to derive from a similar general strategy, on closer observation the courtyard elevation of the Polloni house is of considerably greater complexity. The main openings in the facade are disposed asymmetrically, which is surprising considering the symmetry and axiality announced by the street entrance, with its curved pediment and aedicular entrance gate. The overall plan of the complex is symmetrical. Entering through the gate, one approaches the house on a central axis leading to the entrance door, which is situated in the geometric center of the front facade. However, the central axis and entrance door are disturbingly asymmetrical in relation to a major figural event in the facade, a four-square opening. Marking the entrance, one of the squares, on an axis with and above the entrance, has been further subdivided into four squares responding to the approach. Accepting the axial symmetry of the composition, there is an apparent absence of two additional squares to the right side of the facade center. The missing squares however, are present by implication. A small round window marks the outer edge of the third, missing set of squares. And the apparent lack of two squares is very subtly compensated for by a set of symmetrical, vertical openings that, together with the circular window, recompose the facade. This occult balance produces a frontal surface of unexpected compositional richness. The complexity of the front facade is further elaborated by the fenestration directly behind its surface, the smaller set of four squares on the approach axis overlaying a subdivision of nine squares above the entrance, and the further elaboration of these nine squares into the four nine-square elements surrounding the entrance door. Railings are no longer simply railings, but fenestration without glazing, and thus become an integral part of the orchestration of the vertical surfaces.

The Boni house (1981) is by far the most elaborate of the

Campi·Pessina houses. While it expands the architectural strategies of the Felder and Polloni houses, it seems to search for its expression in the direction of the work of Terragni, rather than in that of the neo-Rationalists. It must also be considered in light of Campi's experiences with American architects and architecture.

The Boni house is located on a steeply sloping site with a magnificent view downhill toward the south. The approach to the site is from a narrow road along its southern edge. The program requirements were extremely complex, involving intricate circulation separating the public from the private and service access to the various parts of the house. Strict zoning and local building restrictions, severely limiting site coverage and building height, required extensive grading and the use of retaining walls, resulting in a succession of terraces following the slope of the ground. Despite these difficulties, the sectional organization of the house is simple. The main part of the house rests on a heavy podium or base, containing a housekeeper's residence, guest rooms, the typical Swiss air raid shelter, wine cellar, and assorted support spaces. The site slopes slightly to the west, allowing the service apartment and guest rooms to have proper exposure and their own private outdoor terrace. The house proper is divided horizontally into two distinct layers, with the social areas of the house at the lower level and the floor above containing bedrooms and other private functions. A stair and an elevator lead to an expansive roof terrace.

Because of the stepped section, on approaching the site one is initially confronted by a large, curved, two-story-high rusticated retaining wall (the base of the house) of carefully laid dark gray marble blocks profusely draped with overhanging plants. The wall is reminiscent, although rendered in a different material, of the type of retaining walls often associated with wine cellars. The carefully composed openings and the choice of material suggest that the base is occupied. Following the curve of the base, one has the first view of part of the white structure of the main house above. What makes the image particularly compelling is the titillating contrast between base and house. This contrast brings to mind such precedents as the Villa dei Vescovi by Giovanni Falconetto, or the Carreto Guido, the Medici villa by Bernardo Buontalenti, with its enormous brick base and access ramps leading to a platform on which the white villa is situated. The dark gray base of the Boni house is a poetic gesture motioning to the rest of the house. In contrast to the historic examples, however, the careful distribution of openings paradoxically transforms the heavy wall of the base into a visually transparent overlay for the entire composition, making it possible to perceive the entire extent of the house.

The contrasts evident in the Boni house are not just those of materials and details, but also those of built form. The architects deliberately juxtapose mass and frame, or cave and hut. The tactile quality of the stone wall presents a pronounced contrast to the seamless, amaterial quality of the white stucco and glass of the house proper. Further, the base wall reveals, through a series of low relief projections, a row of pilasters and arches that give the wall a rhythmical order and suggest the existence of large buttresses, tunnellike voids, or caves behind it, penetrating the slope of the hill.

The entrance to the house is through a gate which, although it is the smallest opening in the base, is immediately identifiable because it is the only vertical opening in the wall. It is further emphasized by an exquisitely detailed, polished white marble frame. The vertical marking of the entrance gate signals the existence of a two-story-high, almost streetlike courtyard, built into the base. The narrow courtyard space of white stuccoed walls focuses on a curved three-story, glass-block screen containing the main entrance door. The courtyard floor of polished black-and-white checkerboard marble is overlaid with a strip of concrete steps which lead, like a rolled-out carpet, to the front door. The finely divided glass-block screen allows a view to the stair hall, visually extending the space of the entrance court through the entire house. The entrance solution invites a comparison to the Polloni house for although both houses are approached on their geometric centers, in the Boni house the relationship of street front to main house is no longer axial, but spatial.

Unlike the two earlier houses, the Boni main house consists essentially of a glass-enclosed structural frame of rectangular columns and beams. As in Terragni's Casa del Fascio, the screenlike frontal surface possesses the unique, ambiguous property of appearing to the a structural grid and, on further viewing solicited by its surface quality—of reading like a cutout wall. The architect even articulates the surface in the same manner as Terragni, through a continuous, deeply cut joint at the back of the front wall. The grid of the front wall has a width of seven equal bays, which are announced by the intervals of the railing and rear wall of the roof terrace. The railings, like triglyphs in a Doric temple, establish the measure of the building. The front wall has been interrupted by the removal of three bays, which register within the facade the two-story volume of the living room. Consequently, the beam over this opening has been doubled in depth, further emphasizing the void. Into this void the architect introduces a separate three-bay-wide structural system of round columns. This grid is slightly smaller than the grid registered by the front surface; it is symmetrically disposed about the opening and moved slightly back of the frontal plane. The main cutout, however, produces an asymmetry in the front facade. In order to recenter the facade, a glass-block screen is introduced that aligns with the central axis of the house and registers on the facade the interior space of primary circulation. The glass-block screen gives clear expression to the living room and establishes a new symmetrically disposed field within the facade. The facade is a brilliant display of compositional displacement and spatial layering.

The system of round columns introduces a space within a space, which since it is three bays wide, has its own center. Like a *baldacchino*, a private study is nested in the center bay, creating a focus that includes the main seating area of the living room just below. The use of round columns as a secondary system within the primary grid of square columns constitutes another subtle juxtaposition, since square columns generally imply static, precisely defined space, while round columns act like spatial vortices and suggest a dynamic composition of space and the free plan. Significantly, all the plastic events within the house are relegated to the space described by the round columns. In a deliberate contrast to the light-filled, airy living room, the theme of the cave and hut is restated by introducing, off to the side of the living room, a windowless fireplace inglenook. The entire plan explores centering and recentering, using devices that are more reminiscent of the early work of Le Corbusier than of Terragni. As in the villa "Les Terraces" at Garches, Campi-Pessina orchestrates its architecture through structure, together with the spatial elements of the plan.

The design for the Gymnasium of the Convent of 1980, a gymnasium for a private school, demonstrates the same subleties and compositional skills displayed in the houses. The building is located adjacent to an earlier building designed by Piazzoli. The gymnasium is not simply a complementary addition, but unites both buildings into one inseperable composition. The design provides a textbook demonstration of contextual responsiveness. Unfortunately, most photographs tend to show the building as an isolated object on a hill site, and thus do not illustrate how the entry facade was composed in concert with the end wall of the existing building. The frontal surfaces of the two buildings align, forming a single plane, and also correspond in height. The facade of the gymnasium is punctured by a set of large openings that produce the effect of a screen behind which the volume of the stairwell is revealed. The large cylinder of the stairwell causes the members of the vertical surface to appear to delineate a delicate cutout in the massive wall. The approach to the entry throws the space between the two buildings into deep perspective, counteracting the forward thrust of the convex stairwell.

Like Le Corbusier and Louis Kahn, Campi·Pessina animate a facade by placing the fenestration alternately at its front and rear surfaces. For the window wall of the Gymnasium the large single panes of glass are kept flush with the outside surface, while the lower part of the windows is subdivided and set back. Between the two surfaces, are devices for ventilation. From the interior of the gymnasium, the lower windows, appearing to project into the space at the level of the players, give an intimate sense of scale, while the large upper windows produce a visual extension of the space to the outside.

The Maggi House (1980) was designed at about the same time as the Gymnasium, but it seems to bear a closer affinity to the Amberg House of 1975, which stands in curious contrast to the rest of their work in making an obvious reference to the vernacular architecture of the region. For many architects, the directness of architectural forms distilled by usage over generations serves as a source of inspiration. Le Corbusier, for example, throughout his life would turn for inspiration to the study of "folklore," as he referred to vernacular architecture. It is worth observing that at the same time Le Corbusier designed and built the Villa Savoye and the Pavillon Suisse, he also designed and built the Maison Weekend, the summer house at Methes, and the Villa Mandrot.

The Maggi house might be seen as a highly sophisticated farm house. The almost temple-like front, however, is a response to a small church on a site opposite it. The downhill facing facade is a simple gable front with two round columns inserted into a large opening. This appears to be a very simple solution, except that the wall behind the columns has four openings, contradicting the divisions in the gable front, and the wall set further back in the volume behind has five divisions. The two peripheral openings of

both inner walls are equal in size and aligned. The layers of the wall in the sequence have single openings which are precisely aligned with the preceding center opening, but these, in turn, end on a pier rather than on a void. The center of the house is a two-story-high living room with two tall columns in the center of the space that frame a pedimented fireplace. It is an interesting reversal. The outer facade is a gable front with two columns inserted into it. The center facade is two columns and the gable front inserted between. This game of juxtaposition exists throughout the house, yet the house retains the simple, beautiful dignity and respose of a country house, ageless qualities existing beyond style.

A discussion of the compositional aspect of Campi·Pessina buildings is necessarily an incomplete description of their qualities. The thoughtfulness of the formal resolutions does not in any way diminish the other layers of consideration present in the designs. It is the purpose of this discussion to hint at the depth and richness of the ideas in several exemplary projects and the degree of sophistication and creative inspiration that makes the work of this firm unique among the "Tendenza" architects.

THE COMMITMENT TO TRADITION

Mario Campi

With the passage of time, every work of architecture comes to be part of both daily life and history, allowing a glimpse of lost chances and forgotten opportunities. If one only indulges in the pleasure of digging among these ruins, unexpected new perspectives open up. Look back to the past, then, once more. But which "past" springs before our eyes and fills our memories? And then, where begins the slow process of recognition? We look to the past to find confirmation of our predilections, our desires to reconstruct our own personal history out of the splinters into which the history of architecture (and the monolithic Modern Movement) has been shattered.

"Personal" but not "new." Even if we have always made reference to the modern project that Jurgen Habermas speaks of, the category "new," in the sense bestowed upon it by the avant-gardists, has been far from our interests. Rather, we have chosen to immerse ourselves in a transformation, more precisely, a revision, of tradition, of modern traditions.

At first our work was strongly characterized by the prevailing sense of experimentation in the 1950s and 1960s, when the influence of Frank Lloyd Wright, Louis Kahn, and Le Corbusier was strongly felt in the Ticino. But slowly, as our first buildings began to rise, and then abandon us, we turned our attention to a certain type of Italian Rationalism, particularly that of Como and Milan. Only a few kilometers and a border—a more or less imaginary line—separated us from buildings already in existence. Even before the war, on this side of the border, in our own Lugano, it was possible to find one important example of this type of Rationalism, the cantonal library by Carlo and Rino Tami, a demonstration of reciprocal influences and shared intentions. Having abandoned our reveries of experiments which were distant and "abstract" in regard to our own context, our focus on a particular historical experience came to coincide with regional and geographical limits.

This approach is consolidated in our project for the restoration of the Montebello Castle in Bellinzona. Here, the desire to establish a dialectical relationship with the existing structure is expressed. The clarity of the new intervention, the structural invention, the rigor of the construction, the search for a simplified language reduced to essentials, the insistence on differences and on specificity—these are constants that have characterized our work from the beginning. These constants also surface in our recent, urban-scaled projects, where our interventions, in sites that are very stratified from a historical viewpoint, are a reproposal of the problems posed in Bellinzona. The interventions are not adapted to the existing situation, rather these conditions are considered an important point of departure.

All this is accompanied by our reclamation of a specific formal legacy as the basis of our work: an abstract language, filtered and reduced to a few, precise elements. We have not shied away from deconstructive or reconstructive operations in our attempt not so much to produce something "new," but to transform tradition from within, even if that tradition is a "modern" one. Furthermore, the choice of "limits" for our area of work has seemed fundamental to our desire to proceed with a critical revision. From the start, we have endeavored not to resolve general problems, but to bring to light the contradictions around us.

The explicit and declared choice of a Rationalist language is not dictated by a desire to exercise virtuosic and rhetorical manipulation of a "dead language." While the modern tradition has somewhat lost its driving ideological force, it does not seem empty to us, but continues to live within architecture, although with meanings different from the original ones. This happens with every tradition. This Rationalist language still possesses its own sense of ethics, internal to the architecture, a morality of construction that ties us not only to the Rationalist experience, but to the artisanal and professional traditions shared by other Ticinese, Domenico Fontana, Francesco Borromini, and Carlo Maderno, among them. Only through the mastery of materials and the recognition of their intrinsic qualities is it possible to translate experience into project, and this into material form.

And so one seeks to give life to things, and to have them speak.

Translated from the Italian by Meg Shore.

Rowhouses, Massagno, Switzerland,
1985. Rear facade detail.

Campo dei Fiori, Lugano, Switzerland,
1983. Interior view.

Boni House. Interior view showing the inside of the front facade.

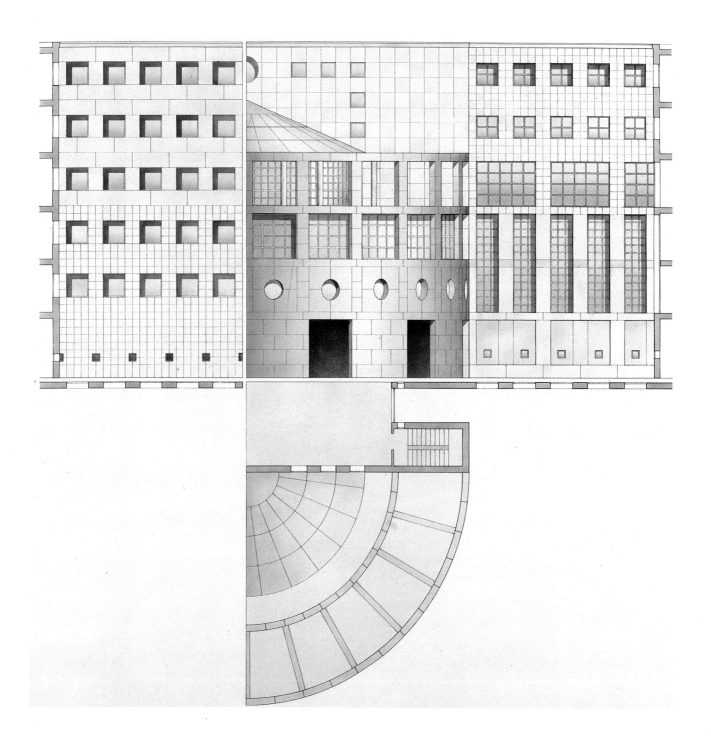

Competition for Gottardo Bank, Lugano, Switzerland, 1983. Composite drawing.

*Swiss National Bank, Lugano,
Switzerland, 1978. Exploded
axonometric and plans.*

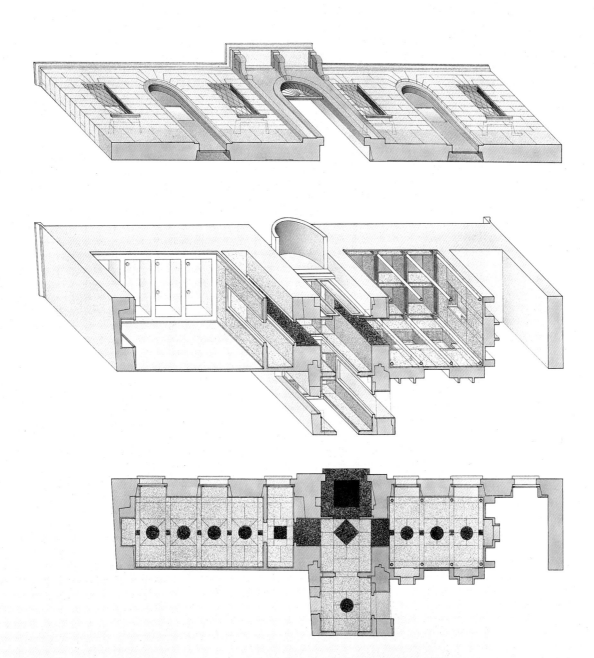

Consortial Schools of the Lower
Malcantone, Caslano, Switzerland,
1975. Gymnasium.

Boni House, Massagno, Switzerland,
1981. Entrance wall detail.

Gymnasium, Neggio, Switzerland,
1980. Stairwell detail.

24

SELECTED BIOGRAPHIES

Mario Campi

1936	Born in Zurich, Switzerland
1960	Diploma, Department of Architecture, Eidgenossische Technische Hochschule, Zurich
1962	Co-founds Mario Campi and Franco Pessina, Architects
1975-85	Teaches at Syracuse University, Cornell University, Harvard University, Rhode Island School of Design, and Eidgenossische Technische Hochschule

Franco Pessina

1933	Born in Lugano, Switzerland
1948-51	School of drafting, Bellinzona
1953-62	Practices independently and in collaboration with various offices in Lugano
1962	Co-founds Mario Campi and Franco Pessina, Architects
1983-85	Instructor, Eidgenossische Technische Hochschule, Zurich, School of Architecture at Nancy, and School of Higher Technical Education, Lugano

Niki Piazzoli

1934	Born in Locarno, Switzerland
1964	Diploma, Department of Architecture, Eidgenossische Technische Hochschule, Zurich
1969-83	Practices with Mario Campi and Franco Pessina
1984-present	Director for Federal Buildings, Sector of Ticino, Grigioni (Graubünden) and Italy

SELECTED BIBLIOGRAPHY

26

Filippini House
A + U (September 1976)

Righetti House
Rivista Tecnica (September 1973)

A + U (September 1976)

Montebello Castle
Rivista Tecnica (June 1974)

Archithese (November 1974)

Werk (May 1975)

Casabella (November 1977)

Werk (January/February 1980)

Decoration International (May/June 1982)

Consortial Schools of the Lower Malcantone
Rivista Tecnica (December 1974)

Amberg House
Rivista Tecnica (December 1974)

Casa Vogue (December 1980)

Steinhausen Competition
Aktuelle Wettbewerbe 4 (1977)

Swiss National Bank
Progressive Architecture (July 1982)

Archithese (January 1983)

A + U (October 1983)

Felder House
Werk (January/February 1980)

Rivista Tecnica (November/December 1980)

Gran Bazaar (July/August 1981)

Progressive Architecture (July 1982)

A + U (November 1982)

Boutique Jeff
Rivista Tecnica (November 1984)

Rosshof Competition
Architektur Wettbewerbe (1979-1983)

Gymnasium of the Convent
Rivista Tecnica (November 1981)

Progressive Architecture (July 1982)
A + U (August 1983)

Maggi House
Rivista Tecnica (February 1982)

Progressive Architecture (July 1982)

A + U (November 1982)

Werk (December 1982)

Casa Vogue (1982)

New York Times (March 1983)

Architektur und Wohnen (January 1985)

Boni House
Progressive Architecture (July 1982)

A + U (November 1982)

Werk (December 1982)

Rivista Tecnica (February 1983)

Häuser (January 1985)

Polloni House
Rivista Tecnica (February 1982)

Decoration International (May/June 1982)

Progressive Architecture (July 1982)

A + U (November 1982)

Werk (December 1982)

Frames (January 1984)

Häuser (January 1985)

Bank of Gottardo Competition
Rivista Tecnica 12 (1982)

Muschaweck House
Daidalos 13 (September 1984)

Campo dei Fiori
Werk (June 1984)

Abitare (November 1984)

Häuser (February 1985)

Housing for the Elderly Competition
Rivista Tecnica 4 (1984)

1973
XV Triennal of Architecture, Milan

1975
Tendenzen: Neure Architektur im
Tessin, ETH, Zurich

1978
Third Biennial of Swiss Art, Winthertur

1982
Traveling Exhibition Pro Helvetia

1983
Projects for Basel, Architectural
Competitions, Basel

1984/1986
Exhibition of the Works and Projects of
CPP, Syracuse University, Syracuse,
Harvard University, Cambridge,
University of Kentucky, Lexington,
Université du Quebec, Montreal,
Columbia University, New York,
Cornell University, Ithaca, University
of Toronto, Toronto, Rensselaer
Polytechnic Institute, Troy

27

Vanzini House. Model

BUILDINGS/PROJECTS
1962-1986

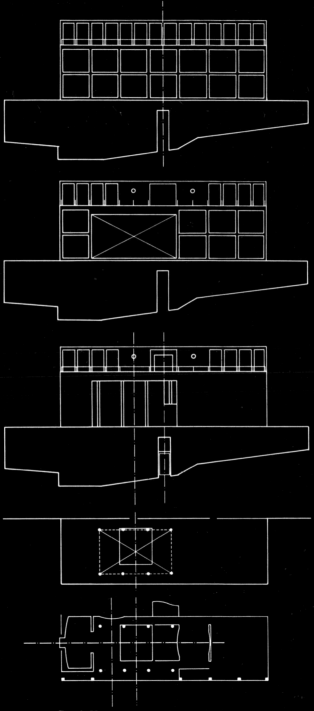

Boni House, 1981. Analytical drawings showing axial relationships.

VANINI HOUSE

Muzzano, Switzerland   1962

1

1 South facade.
2 East facade, detail showing dining room.
3 South facade, detail.

2

3

4 Interior view of upper level on axis with entry.
5 Interior view from living room.
6 Section.
7 View from living room to fireplace.

32 The Vanini house was the first single-family house that the firm realized. Its plan derived from the centrifugal organization of the dwelling spaces around the core of the house. The central living volume is represented by a reinterpretation of the traditional fireplace of the Ticino region. The influence of Louis Kahn is very evident in the spatial articulation which is broken up as much as possible into a series of closed cells.

The livingroom to the south, the diningroom to the west, the bedrooms to the east, and the services to the north are like four hollow pilasters forming the arms of a cross in plan. This plan form was adopted to create a clear spatial continuity and sequence of spaces.

4

5

6

7

Vanini House

8 *Lower level plan.*
9 *Upper level plan.*

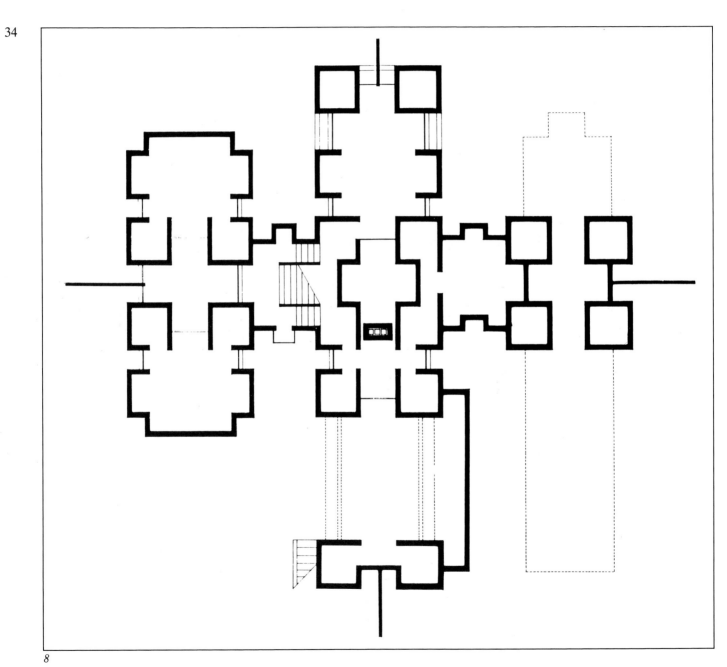

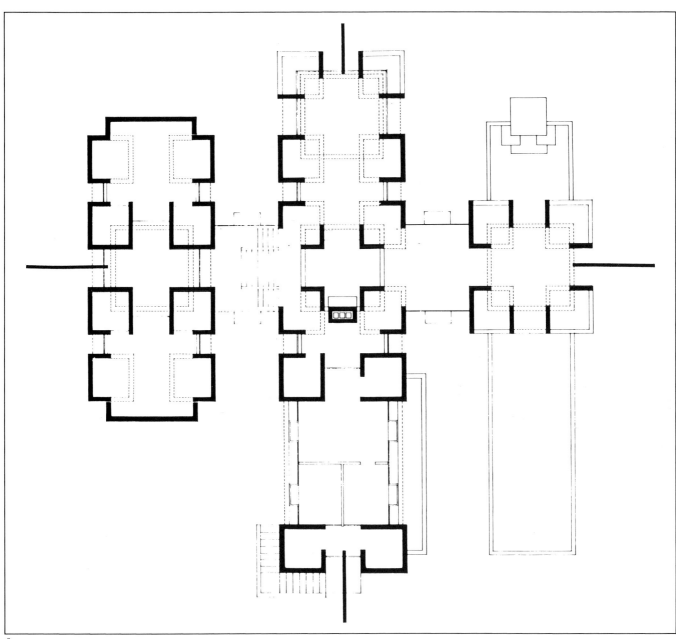

FILIPPINI HOUSE

Muzzano, Switzerland   1964

1

2

1 South facade, view of entrance.
2 South elevation.
3 East facade.
4 View from garden to upper living
room and bedroom.

3

4

This house responds to its site in a particularly emphatic way. The very narrow, long site, the location of an ancient quarry, is bordered on the west by a high rock wall and on the east by a public thoroughfare. This unusual circumstance provides the setting for the house of a renowned painter-writer.

The plan is a stretched and elongated rectangle, which is divided into two parts: the artist's atelier and his apartment. The double-height atelier, a perfect cube, faces north; beneath, a showroom is provided for the display of paintings. In response to the configuration of the site, a series of hanging gardens faces toward the south. The narrowness of the house as well as of the site is underlined by the transparency of the entrance facing the quarry wall. The house is opened still further to the quarry by means of a long series of windows, which look out upon the rock. The street facade was kept as opaque as possible to provide privacy as well as a shield against street noise. A *passerelle*, which bridges over the main entrance, connects and interlocks the atelier to the apartment. The dining-room space opens to a balcony, which enjoys a view of the town of Muzzano.

37

Filippini House

5 Top: groud floor plan; middle: first floor plan; bottom: second floor plan.
6 Sections.
7 Axonometric.

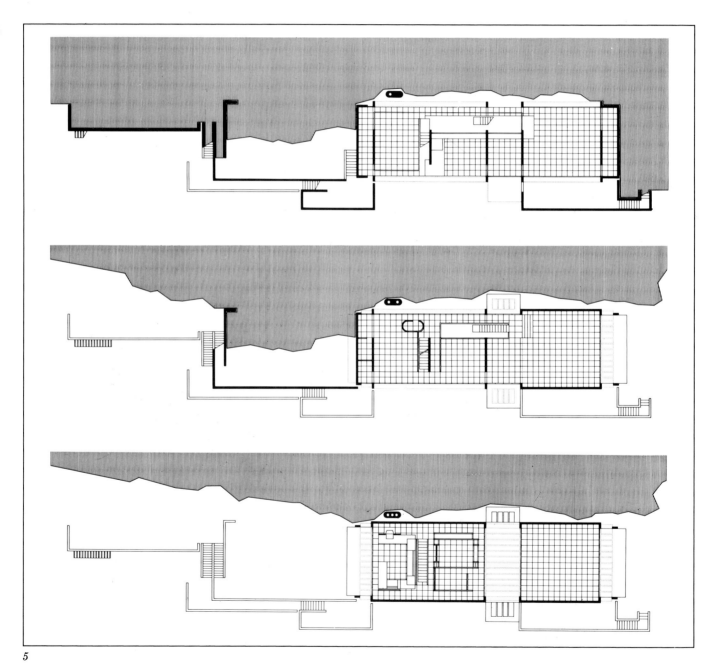

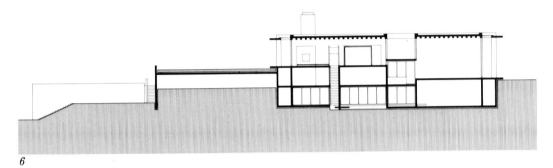

6

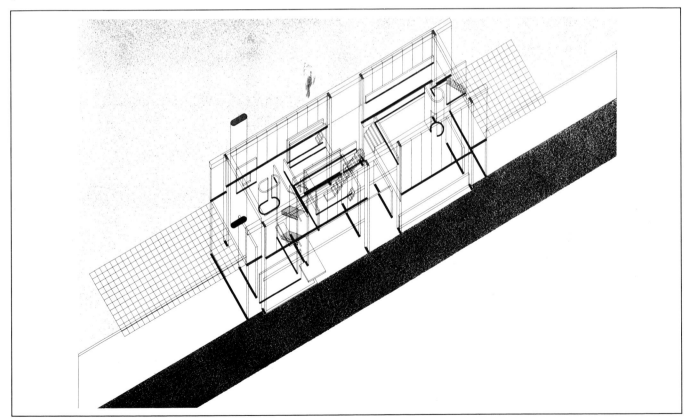

7

Filippini House

*8 Interior view over dining room to
main living space/studio.
9 Fireplace in upper living room.*

40

8

9

10 *Interior corridor.*

RIGHETTI HOUSE

Sorengo, Switzerland   1970

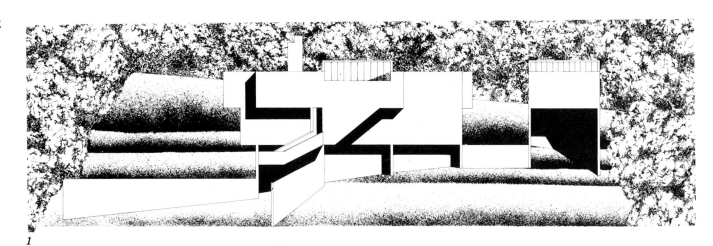

1

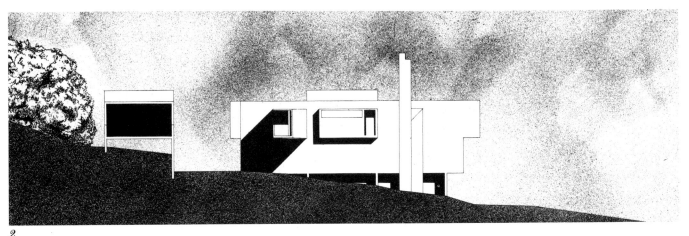

2

This unbuilt design arose out of a particular response to the program in relation to the specific topographical and environmental conditions of the site, including an awkward orientation and a somewhat demanding and difficult architectural context.

The bearing walls are disposed orthogonally to the steep slope of the hill at the ground level, so as to clearly indicate the topographical context. On top of these bearing walls are two longitudinal walls with very few openings. These walls are oriented along the main axis of the house and contain the dwelling volumes. A diagonal stairway leading up to the main entry, and the gentle access ramp are among the main architectural elements that tie the house into the site.

Righetti House

1 *Front elevation.*
2 *Side elevation.*
3 *Cross section.*
4 *Lower level plan.*
5,6 *Side elevations.*

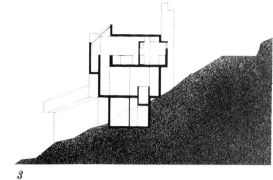

3

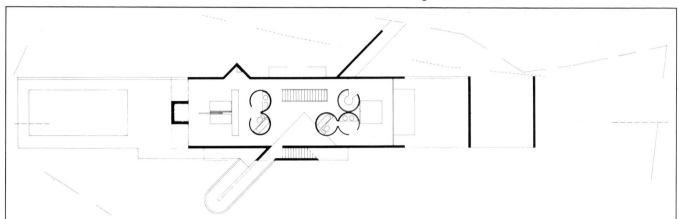

4

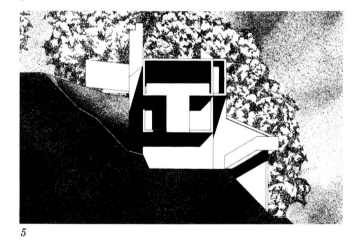

5

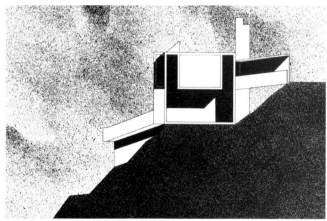

6

MONTEBELLO CASTLE

Bellinzona, Switzerland 1974

44

1

2

1 *Exterior view, detail.*
2 *Interior courtyard.*
3 *Lower level plan.*

The program for this project called for the complete restoration of the medieval Castle of Montebello and its conversion into an archeological museum housing a permanent exhibition of artifacts of the Ticino region in the tower of the castle, with galleries designed for temporary exhibitions located in the contiguous space of the palace.

In the old entry portico and connecting passage between palace and tower, the rigid, simple geometry of concrete slabs provides a counterpoint to the complex forms and materials of the walls and floor. The new stairs and floor slabs are clearly lifted up off the old surfaces, which are revealed as supports and signal the presence of the old building. Suspended from the top of the old tower walls, challenging the immense pressure of this inert mass over its entire height, the new metallic structure fills the hollow space of the tower; a balance is struck between the architecture of restoration and the integrity of the castle's ancient structure.

The museum is an unbroken sequence of short runs from one stair landing to the next, the parenthesis of a single flight marking the rhythm of the ascent. A spiral railing rises to the belvedere, from where a view can be had of the surrounding landscape and excavation sites—a tangible purview of the geographical and archeological terrain.

45

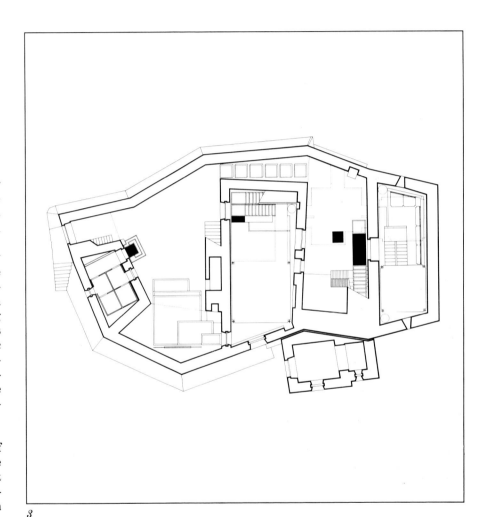

3

46

4

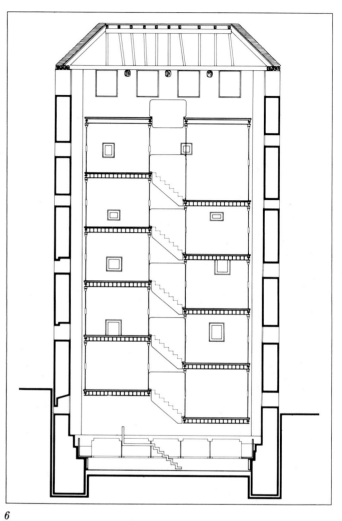

6

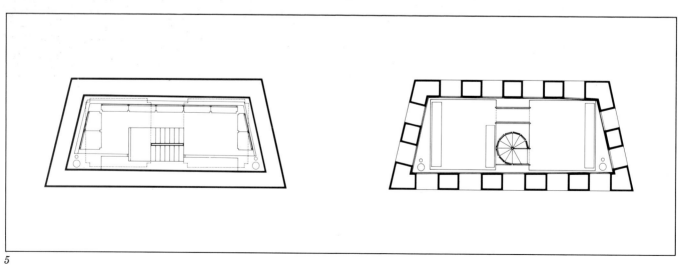

5

Montebello Castle

4 Model view of the structure inserted into the existing tower.
5 Left: lower level plan; right: top level plan.
6 Tower section.
7 Exhibition area in the tower, detail.

7

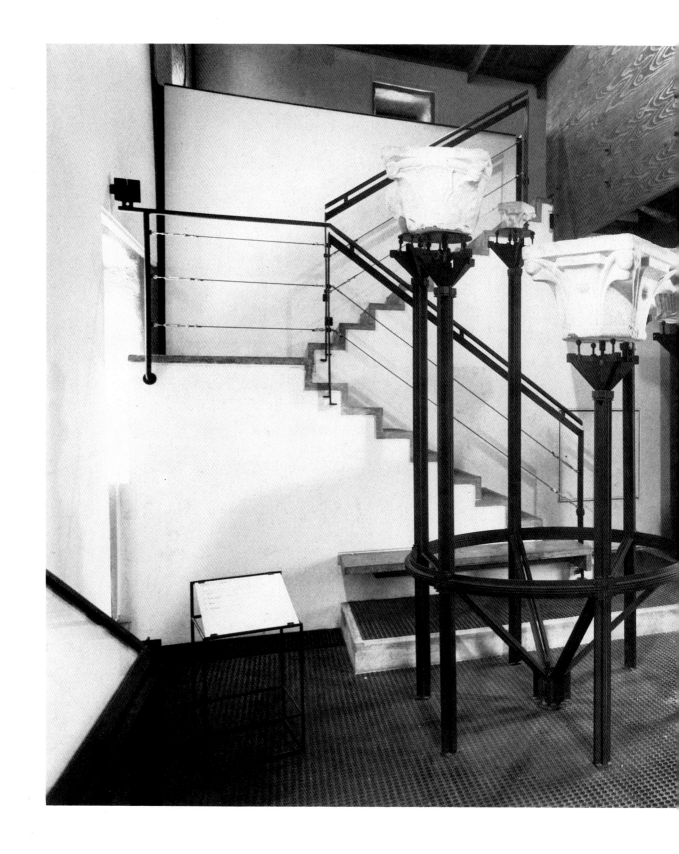

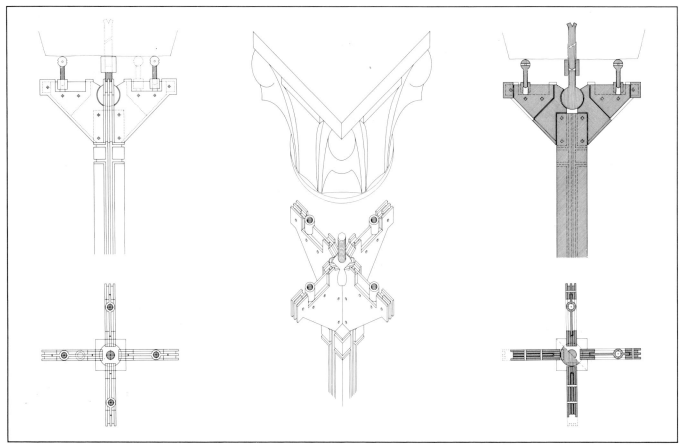

8

9

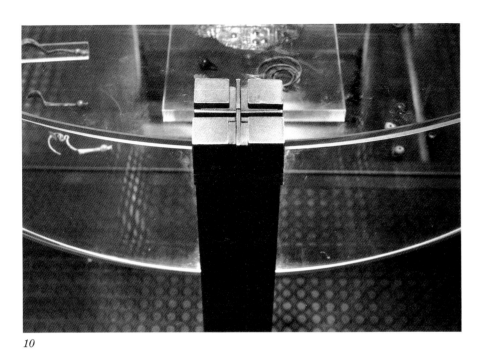

10

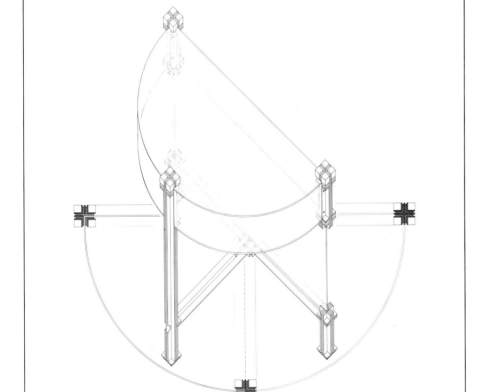

11

12

Montebello Castle

8 Exhibition structure details.
9 Entrance.
10 Exhibition showcase, detail.
11 Detail drawing of the showcase at the turning point of the tower stairs.
12 Stair detail.

51

CONSORTIAL SCHOOLS OF THE
LOWER MALCANTONE

Caslano, Switzerland   1975

1

The design approach for this building was determined principally by three factors: its relationship to the urban context, the articulation of the interior spaces, and the organization of the classrooms.

Relationship to the urban context.
The school is placed in the center of a plain behind Caslano that is characterized by a large variety of interventions—tiny villas, small apartment houses, low buildings, storage buildings, and so forth—that have been inserted into a fairly rigid and simple urban fabric, defined by the traverse of orthogonal district roads.

Despite its meagre massing in relation to the vast site, the building attempts to give as well as suggest order and rhythm to its surroundings, through the mediation of the geometry of its structures, their repetition, and the simplicity of their forms. The volume appears to be abruptly interrupted, suggesting future extensions, like a spine reaching toward the urban space.

Articulation of the interior spaces.
While the building extends itself into the locale, the latter is also led into the interior. The expansive interior space contrasts with the compact exterior volume, alternating with the open spaces of patios. The spatial and functional organization is rigorous and repetitive; the central corridor is reached through the entrance atrium, from which one is led to the classrooms by means of three staircases, which also contain wardrobes and services. These three staircase-wardrobe-service volumes define two interior patios, which give light and air to the in-

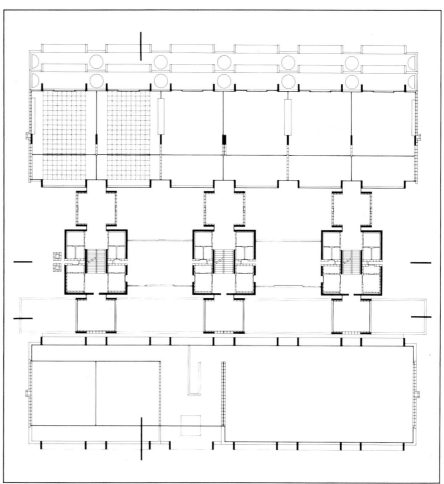

53

2

Consortial Schools

3 East facade, detail.
4 Entrance facade, detail.

3

ternal rooms, the classrooms and library, as well as to the workrooms in front of the classrooms.

Organization of the teaching spaces.
The classrooms are distributed over two levels, and adjacent classrooms are divided by modular, interchangeable panels; this allows for the free disposition of classroom spaces, eliminating the traditional concept of the closed classroom. The space in front of each classroom is conceived as a workspace and is separated from the classroom by sliding panels, that permit the extension of the teaching space into the workspace. The flexibility of the teaching spaces is thus comprehensive, from one classroom to the other, as well as from each classroom to its workspace.

4

Consortial Schools

5 Gymnasium.
6 Classroom.
7 Entrance foyer.
8 Interior corridor.
9 Stair.

56

5

6

8

7

9

STEINHAUSEN COMPETITION

Steinhausen, Switzerland   1977

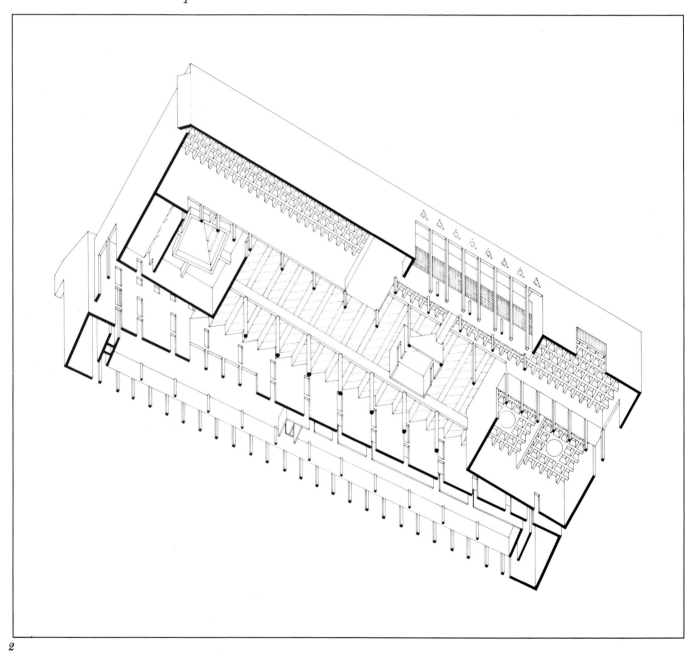

1

2

1 East facade.
2 Axonometric view from below.
3 Site plan.

The site for this project is located in Steinhausen, near Zurich, in the German-speaking region of Switzerland.

The program required an ecumenical center in which visitors could find a Roman Catholic church and chapel, a Protestant chapel with classrooms close by, a library, several rooms for the young people of the Steinhausen community, some offices, and housing for the two clerics.

In addition, it was required that all the public rooms, and in fact all the different spaces, have the capacity for being converted into one huge, continuous room, to be used for festivities held for the entire ecumenical community of Steinhausen.

The site for the center is in a development area of the municipality of Steinhausen and is surrounded on three sides by recently built structures, mostly housing, whereas the fourth side faces an important architectural monument from the seventeenth century: a church, the church's cemetery, which had to be displaced to outside the town as a condition of the competition program, and a charnel-house.

The subsequent analysis of the competition area showed two significant directions: the longitudinal main axis of the existing church, and the main axis of the new housing development around the competition area.

Thus, by acknowledging these two main axes, which are not parallel, we were able to define a project that related to existing conditions.

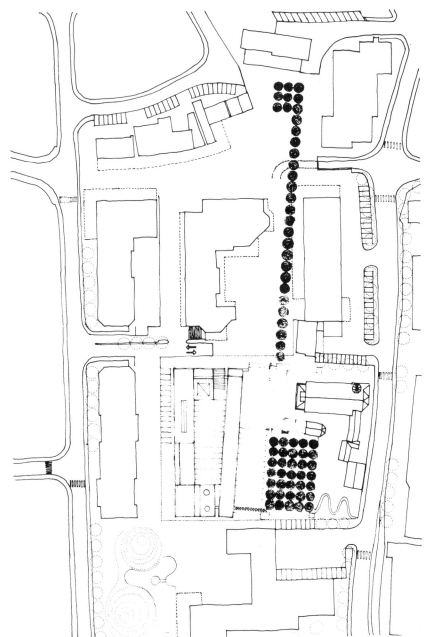

3

60

3

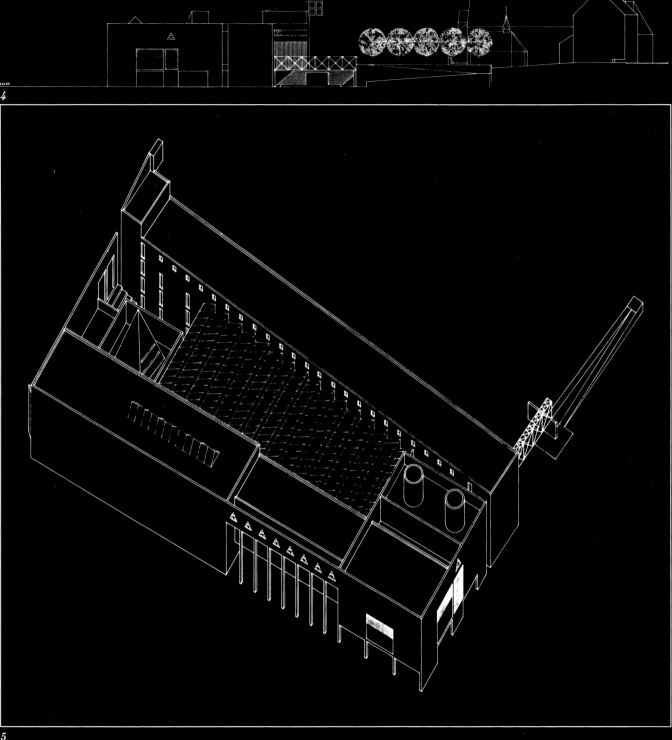

4

5

SWISS NATIONAL BANK

Lugano, Switzerland   1978

62

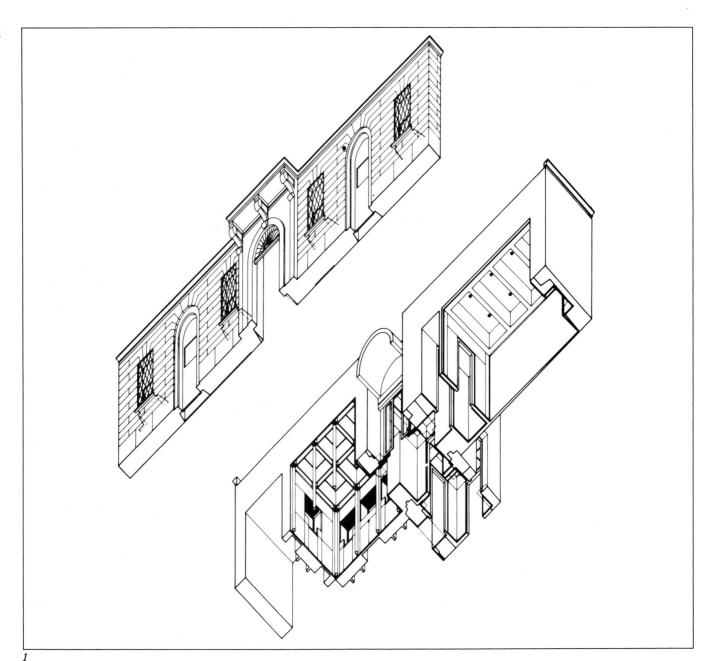

1

The program for this project called for re-modeling the entrance, conference, and banking rooms in the Swiss National Bank in Lugano.

The building that houses the National Bank was built in the middle of the eighteenth century by Albertolli as his own residence. It was conceived as a simple three-story-high prism with a rusticated base. Our intention was to have the small ground floor rooms, which have a width of approximately nine feet, appear larger than their actual size. To this end, reflective materials were used: the walls, the columns, and the "beams" in the banking room are made of white, highly polished marble, and the floor of black and white marble; the fields between the "beams" are made of light blue glass and appear, through backlighting, to be a sky that "dissolves" the ceiling.

The choice of materials had expected as well as unexpected results—the reflections created a surreal space.

The architectural language of these spaces contains elements from the history of architecture—columns, capitals, and so forth—that relate to the original building. These elements are reduced to minimalist terms, which gives the design, although differentiated by the function of the spaces, a strong sense of stillness.

2

3

Swiss National Bank

4 Plan.
5 Section.
6 Column/ceiling joint detail.

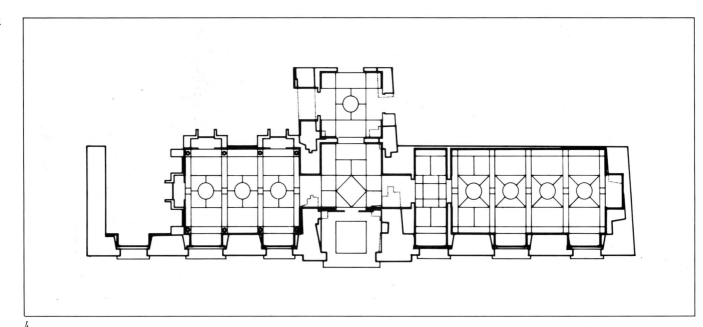

4

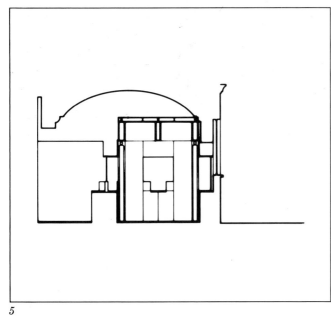

5

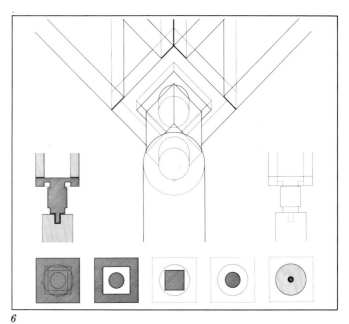

6

7

FELDER HOUSE

Lugano, Switzerland 1978

1

2

3

The Felder House is located on top of a 67
hill overlooking Lake Lugano, below a
late-eighteenth-century villa, the Palazzo Riva, that was the catalyst for
many aspects of the design approach. In
particular, the siting and typological references of the Felder House represent
the reuse of many architectural concepts
intrinsic to the courtyard house already
existing on the site. The Felder House
shows, as a result, a siting and attitude
toward the landscape similar to that of
the palazzo. Its architectural language
relates to some of the architecture of the
1920s and 1930s that can be found around
the lakes of the Lombardia region.

Parallels also exist with Roman courtyard houses, and with the successive
transformations and evolutions of the
courtyard as a type. Different space-
making elements are used to generate
the design of the house. Spatially, the
courtyard and screen wall fronting it act
as a two-way system: as an actual extension of the house and a conceptual extension, in reaching out to nature, of its
living spaces, and as the elements that
capture the landscape and bring it closer
to the house, producing a dynamic relationship between the two.

The U-shaped plan creates separate
zones for parent's and and childrens' bedrooms on opposite sides of the courtyard.

Felder House

4 *Lower level plan.*
5 *Left: cross section; right: longitudinal section.*
6 *Upper level plan.*
7 *Courtyard view.*
8 *View of living room and courtyard.*

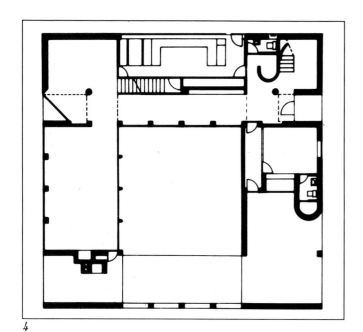

4

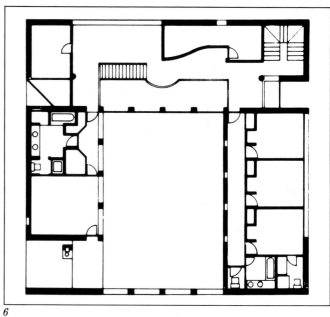

6

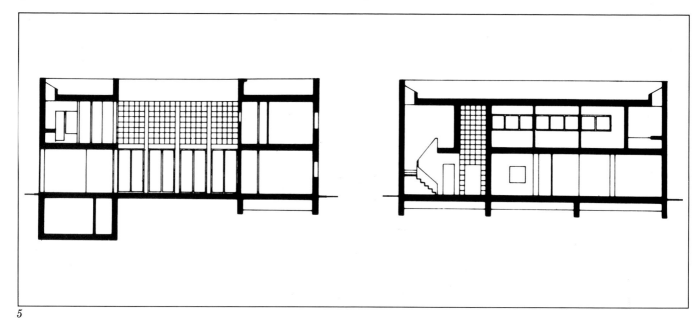

5

7

8

Felder House

9 Interior view from upper level, over entrance.
10 Interior view towards entrance.

9

ROSSHOF COMPETITION

Basel, Switzerland   1979

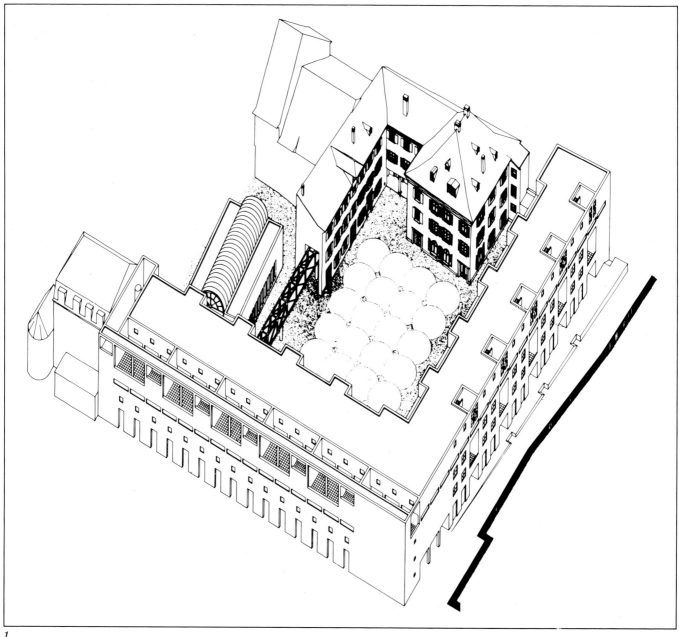

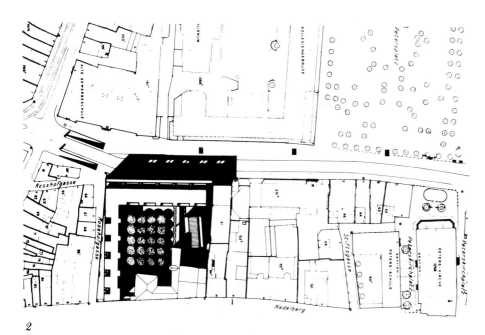

2

3

In this design we attempted to integrate as well as interpret the preliminary analysis of the site. Incorporated into the theme of the project are the qualities of the topography and the built context, especially in terms of its historical layerings.

The courtyard type employed in the design constitutes, on the one hand, a built extension of the Rosshof building; on the other hand, it attempts to emphasize the significance of the building in terms of its public value for the city. The building will be a communal dwelling, in addition to accommodating craft studios and shops and secondary activities for the university.

The design further attempts to continue the housing tradition on the Nadelberg. Thus, it simultaneously represents a closed entity, one that encompasses the existing structures (Rosshof, Schöner Hof, Peterskirche) as important elements of urban design. In this way it underlines the idea of continuity and confrontation between old and new.

73

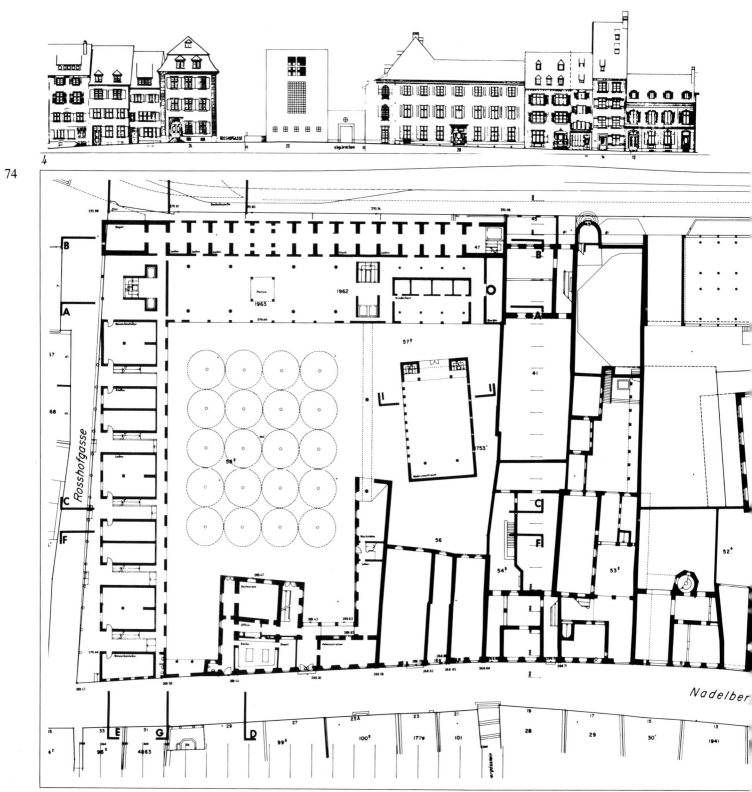

4

5

Rosshofgasse

Nadelber

4 *East elevation.*
5 *Ground floor plan, in street context.*

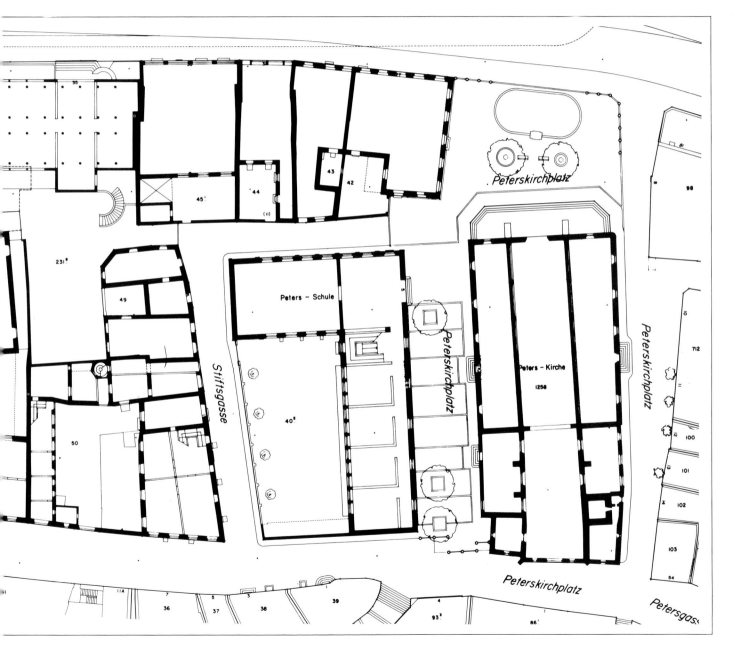

BOUTIQUE JEFF

Lugano, Switzerland   1979

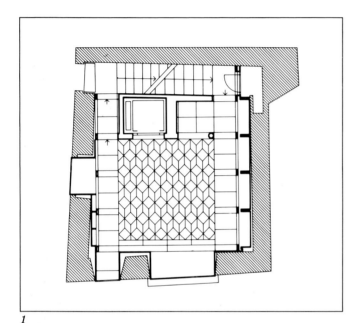

1

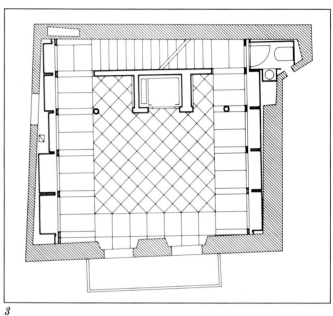

3

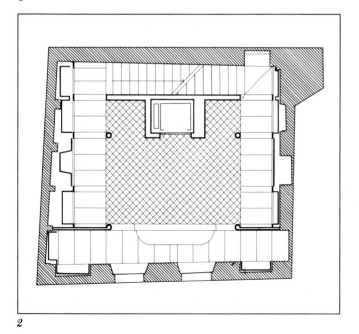

2

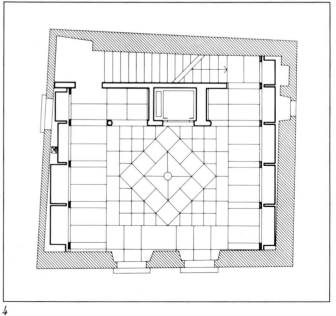

4

1 *Ground floor plan.*
2 *First floor plan.*
3 *Second floor plan.*
4 *Third floor plan.*
5 *Renovated entrance facade.*

The design of the Boutique Jeff is characterized by a series of restricting premises: the existing building's structural system of old concrete floors, the spans of which are integrated with the columns, as well as previous interventions intended to stabilize the structure with reinforced concrete.

The sales areas are distributed over various floors, forming a sequence that starts at the top floor and descends. The new insertions—the staircase, the new lining of the elevator, and the columns—constitute an object within an object, one that is characterized by lacquered, shining surfaces. The other surfaces act as counterparts to these: the regularized enclosure panels and the ceiling are opaque, the shelving conceived to display the objects is constructed of marble panels that are attached in such a manner as to suggest the idea of space cut into encrustations, and multicolored marbles in motifs that recall the sixteenth century make up the floor paving, which indicate a path alongside the shelves.

Mirrors are inserted into the vanities of the bar with the intention of spatially multiplying the restricted space and are attached to the flanks of the elevator in an attempt to dematerialize its disturbing volume.

As with the Swiss National Bank project, this boutique attempts to geometricize the small, irregular rooms of an existing, historic building. The resulting residual spaces are then used to meet functional needs, such as vertical circulation, and to emphasize the architectural and spatial articulation through load-bearing, space-defining elements.

5

78

GYMNASIUM OF THE CONVENT

Neggio, Switzerland   1980

1

The gymnasium was commissioned by the Fondazione Soldati, a private organization directed by the canton of Ticino. It is set into a steeply sloping site, and adjoins the Villa Soldati and a dormitory built in 1969. Its layout is economical, with the area of each floor being not much greater than that of the standard playing court that occupies nearly the whole of the first floor (the ground and second floors house offices, locker rooms, and smaller gym rooms).

The front elevation of the concrete volume was designed as a mask or entry piece that establishes various spatial readings. The outer surface of the wall is marked by the large, square second-floor window over the entrance, which is flush with the facade, while the six small windows flanking it are set in slightly. Set further back from the mask is a white stucco cylinder containing a steel stair that winds its way around a triangular void. The openings to the sides of the cylinder reveal the deep space of the entryway.

On the main playing floor, standard steel beams span the ceiling, while a long, narrow skylight illuminates the opposite (blank) wall, and steel windows dominate one side of the building. The windows, which can be interpreted as giant-scale variants of the classic double-hung window, turn the playing court into a loggia that is flooded with natural light.

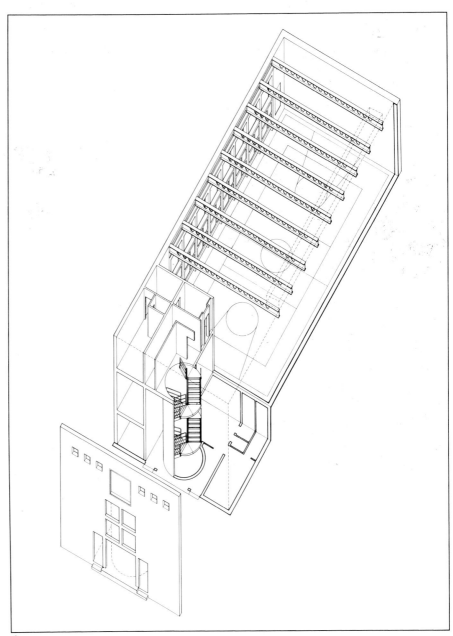

81

2

Gymnasium

3 Entrance facade.
4 North facade.
5 Rear view.

3

4

5

6 Top: ground floor plan; middle: first floor plan; second floor plan. bottom: roof plan.

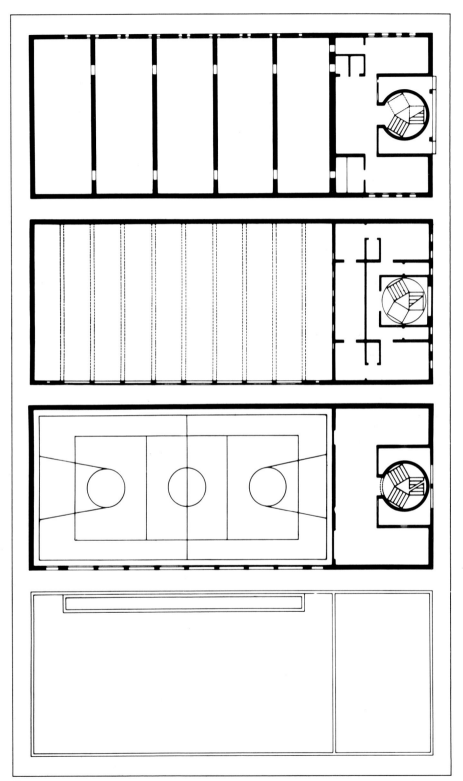

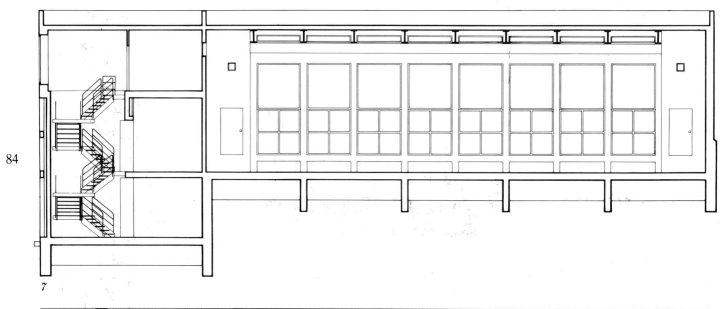

7

8

Gymnasium

7 Longitudinal section.
8 Staircase detail, view from inside.
9 View through the gymnasium
windows.

9

MAGGI HOUSE

Arosio, Switzerland   1980

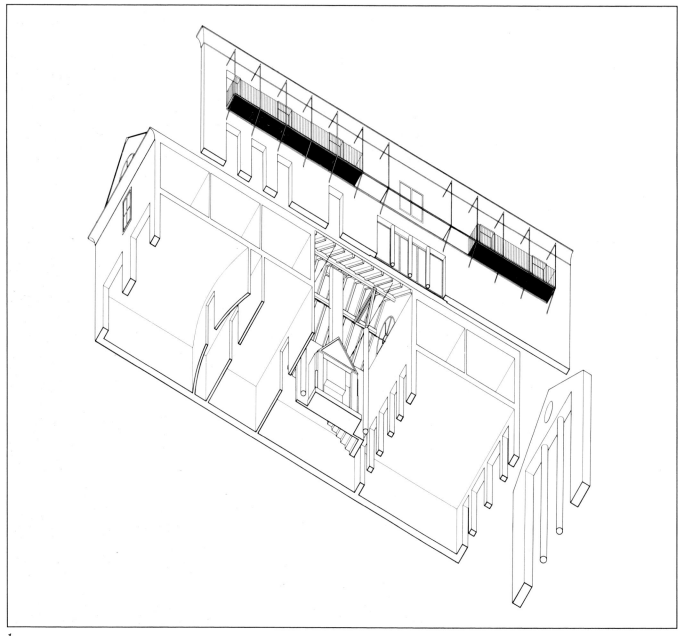

1 Axonometric.
2 Front facade.

The Maggi House is an exercise in rural contextualism. Built in the town of Arosio for the owner of a construction company, the house is set into a hill facing a church. It is a long parallelpiped prism that can be crossed lengthwise on two levels. On the lower level it can be traversed through the sequence of the various daytime living spaces, and on the upper level by the long corridor that serves as the nighttime sleeping quarters.

The house with its temple-like front placed on axis with the church's campanile, sets up a meeting of the sacred and the secular. The white stucco walls are enclosed by an attached, quarter-round cornice derived from those typical of Ticinese chapels. The gabled roof, required by zoning regulations, precipitated our efforts to deal with the historical context of the small village. The simple containerlike quality of the house announces the spaces it contains through the sequence of its openings which are related to the house's near and distant landscapes.

The massive, almost schematic facade, with its concrete pediment and columns, was designed as a mask to cut off the long rectangular volume of the house itself. This detached facade symbolizes memory and representation as it faces the historical village. Rather than making a smooth transition from mass to mask, the house is deliberately sliced off leaving its cornice to stop short, exaggerating the physical and conceptual gap between house and facade.

2

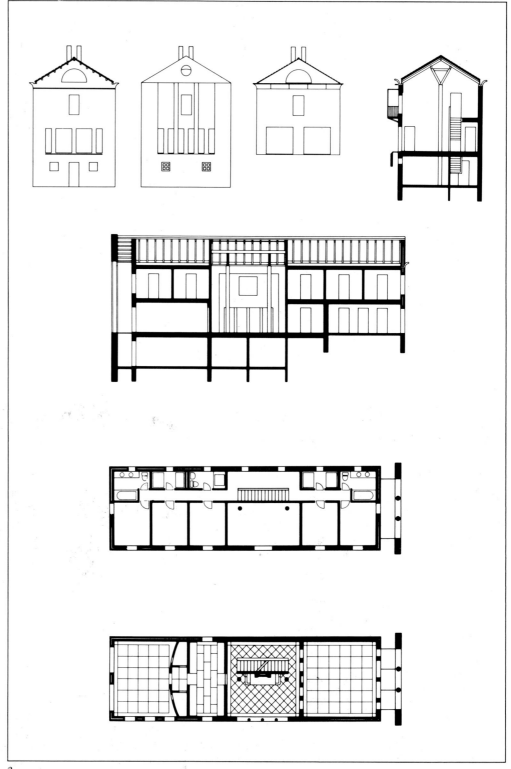

Maggi House

3 Front facades, cross section,
longitudunal section, lower level and
upper level plans.
4 Southeast facade.
5 Terrace detail.
6 North facade.
7 Southeast view.

4

6

5

7

Maggi House

8 Dining room and the "house of fire."

8

9 Interior view of roof structure.
10 View from living room

9

10

BONI HOUSE

Massagno, Switzerland   1981

1

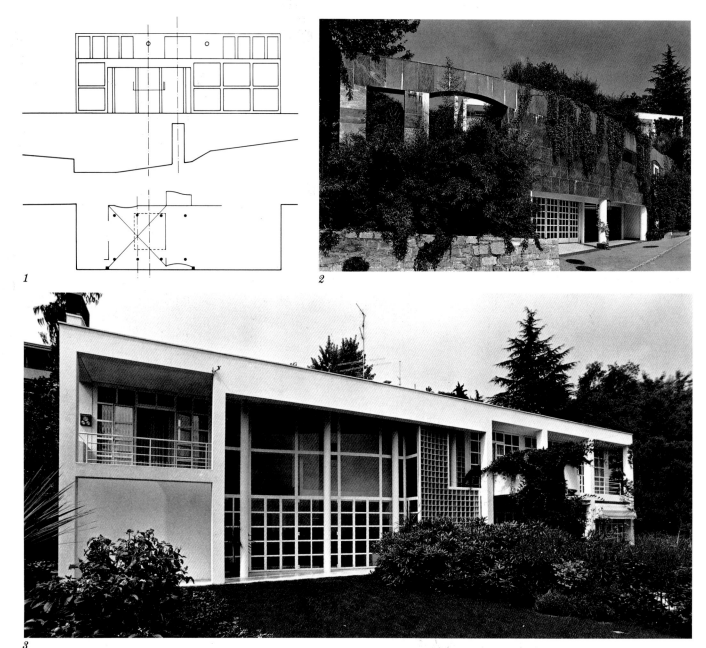

2

3

1 *Analytical drawing detail showing*
axial relationships.
2 *Retaining wall, showing entrance.*
3 *Front facade.*
4,5 *Axonometrics.*

The Boni House is a large single-family house with an adjoining apartment for the caretaker on the lower level. It was designed as an artifact sitting atop a wall. The house has a very complex program of interior spaces related to each other by a triple system of internal circulation. There is a formal entry that leads up to the entrance door, while a secondary entry serves the caretaker's apartment. The primary entryway is extended to bridge over the honorific entry path, thus approaching the house in a somewhat seclusive way, while also isolating the traffic to the childrens' rooms.

The very prestigious site overlooks Lake Lugano in the distance. Thus, all the spaces in the house were oriented toward the view, while all the services (bathrooms, storage, etc.) form a layer at the back of the house, that acts as a buffer against the noise of the street above the site. The garden above the front wall and in front of the main volume of the house allows for a very quiet and private outdoor living space. The materials chosen for the interior, white walls and ceilings, and light grey marble for the floors, are intended to accommodate the exhibition of artworks by the client, a collector.

In designing the front facade, we have been very influenced by Giuseppe Terragni. In fact, the facade can be considered to be an hommage to Terragni.

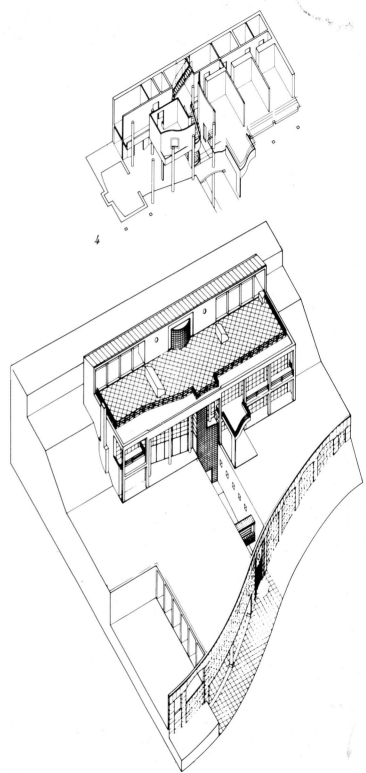

4

5

Boni House

5 Entrance gate.
*6 View from balcony across the main
facade.*
7 Rear view.

5

6

7

8 Entrance detail.

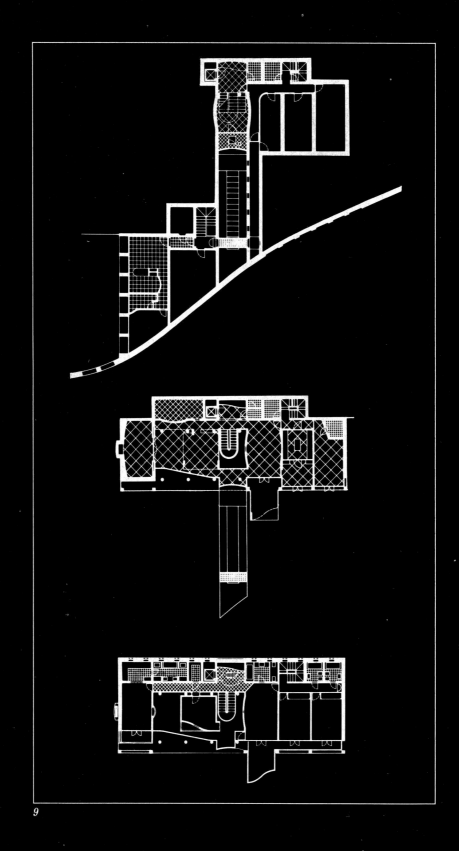

Boni House

9 Top and middle: lower level plans;
 bottom: upper level plan.
10 Top: cross section; middle:
 longitudinal section; bottom: elevations.

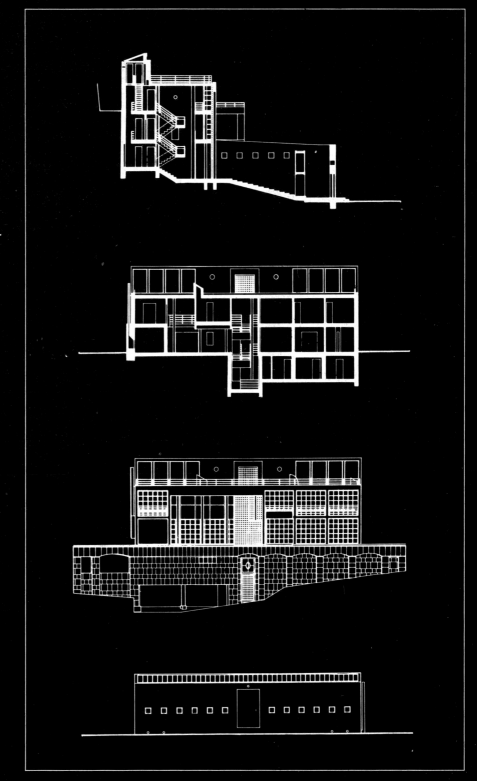

Boni House

11 *View looking up stairwell.*
12 *Staircase at upper level.*

11

12

13 Living room.
14 Sitting room with fireplace.
15 View from top landing.
16 View from staircase looking out.

13

15

14

16

POLLONI HOUSE

Origlio, Switzerland   1981

1

1 *Front facade.*
2 *Axonometric.*
3 *Entrance gate.*

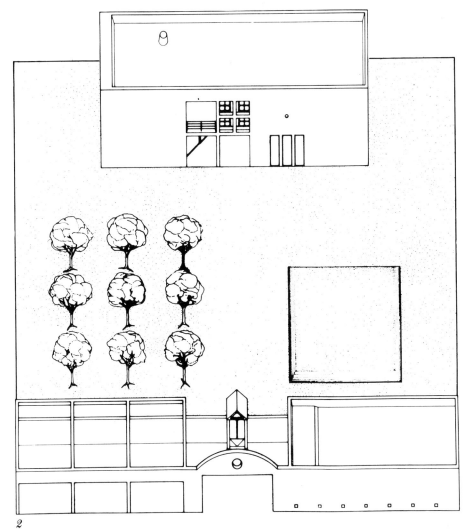

2

3

The Polloni House, like most of our work, was designed to accommodate its surroundings. In some of our buildings, the form arises out of a synthesis of positive relations to the environment. In other cases, the pressure which is exerted by the surroundings on a given site may be experienced negatively. The latter is the case with the Polloni House, located near Lugano. The street that runs along the site is not a very busy one. Nevertheless it became an element to be considered because of the poor architectural quality and siting of the buildings flanking the street.

Our proposal to the client was to separate the private garden space from the street by erecting a long wall-like structure along the street. This allows for privacy in the garden and the house, a basic and desirable quality of life in the countryside.

This approach led us to place the house at the far end of the site, opposite the wall. The garden thus simultaneously divides and connects the house and the wall. Hence the garden becomes a quiet and calm space for all domestic activities.

Polloni House

4 Entrance door.
5 Entrance gate and garage.
6 View across entry space on upper level.
7 Sections.
8 Bottom and middle: lower level plans; top: upper level plans.

102

4

5

6

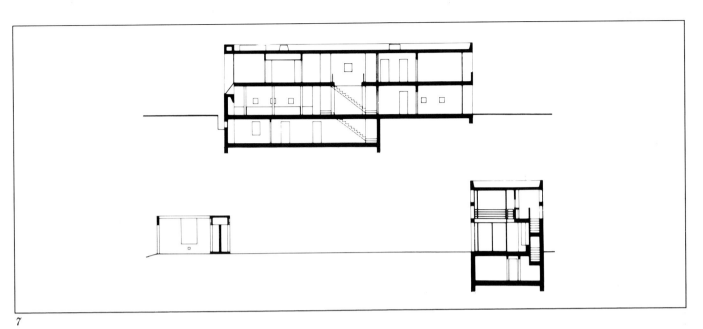

7

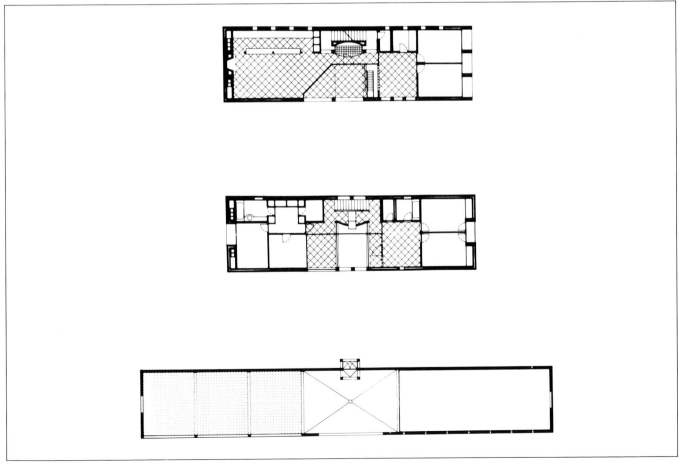

8

9

10

Polloni House

9 Dining room.
10 View from living room to dining room.
11 View from study to bedroom.

11

CAMPO DEI FIORI

Lugano, Switzerland   1983

106 In this project we converted a very small, irregular space in an existing historical building in the center of Lugano into a geometricized space, with the residual areas being used for service spaces, such as storage rooms. Additionally, we wanted to emphasize the architectural meaning and issues of the shop by means of space-defining elements, such as the metal grid used on the walls and ceiling and the two-color marble floors.

In other words, we wanted to render what had until then been only volume into spatial substance.

The space is divided into halves by a perfectly symmetrical axis. This axis ends in a circular shaped wall made of backlit translucent milkglass and is emphasized by the sales counter, a white marble plate resting on a base of mirrors and a slim marble and steel column, the whole like a piece of jewelry.

Mirrors fill in the fields of the grid and create new, unexpected, spaces that come and go with each displacement of the onlooker. The countless references of the reflections constitute a space, the irreality of which is emphasized by the converging dynamic of the parallel lines of the grid.

1

2

1 Store front.
2 Interior view with fountain.
3 Top left: section; bottom left:
elevation; top right: plan.

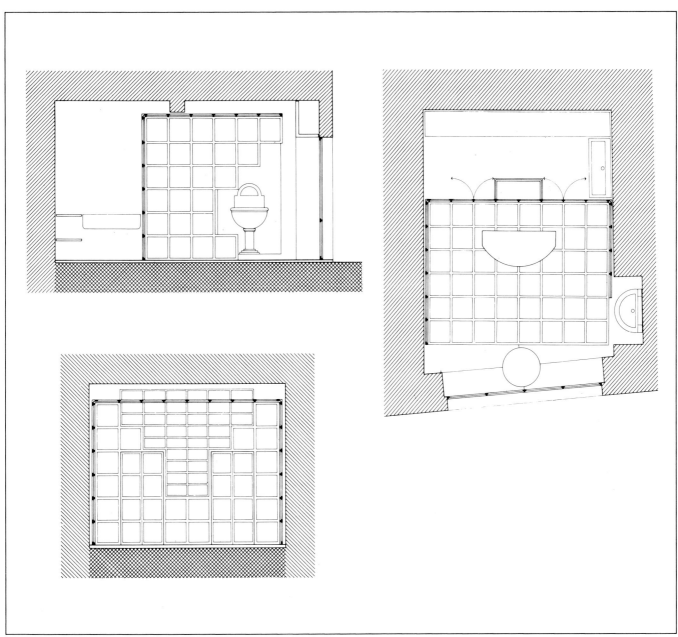

Campo dei Fiori

1 Interior view

MUSCHAWECK HOUSE

Carabbietta, Switzerland   1984

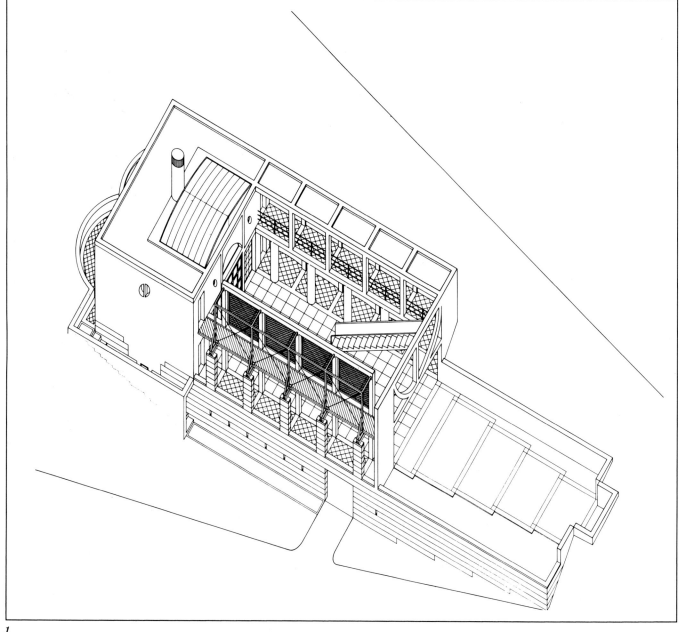

1 Axonometric.
2 Lower level plan.
3 Upper level plan

111

In our design for the Muschaweck House, we attempted to find a new use for the classical type of the "half courtyard" which can be found in the *palazzi* on the Alpine lakes. It is here given a new interpretation relating to the local climate and regional characteristics.

Although the house is relatively small, it is meant to stand out from its surroundings and to acquire a prominent status. For that reason we have organized the garden/courtyard in such a way as to expand the space and have the building conform to the idea of a house that is fixed in its place in a particular way. To achieve this we used a familiar scheme: on one of its facades the house makes a public contribution to its immediate surroundings, on the other it has private advantages for the users.

The axonometric drawing clearly expresses the design intentions. The manifestly overscaled portal on the far side of the courtyard is the public tribute that the house pays to its environment. It is designed to establish visually the building axis in relation to the courtyard. It also clearly establishes the continuity between a constructed nature and the natural landscape, relating the surrounding space, that is, everything beyond the courtyard, to the house. At the same time, the portal invites the environment to accept the house, thus overcoming the threshold. The portal is located in the exact place where the architecture of the house becomes a monument to the place.

The highly intimate, private character of the house is expressed inside the courtyard. This is a place articulated by its

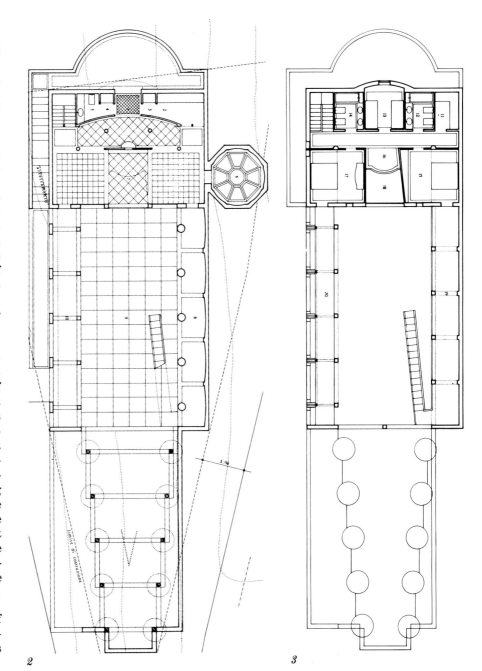

2   3

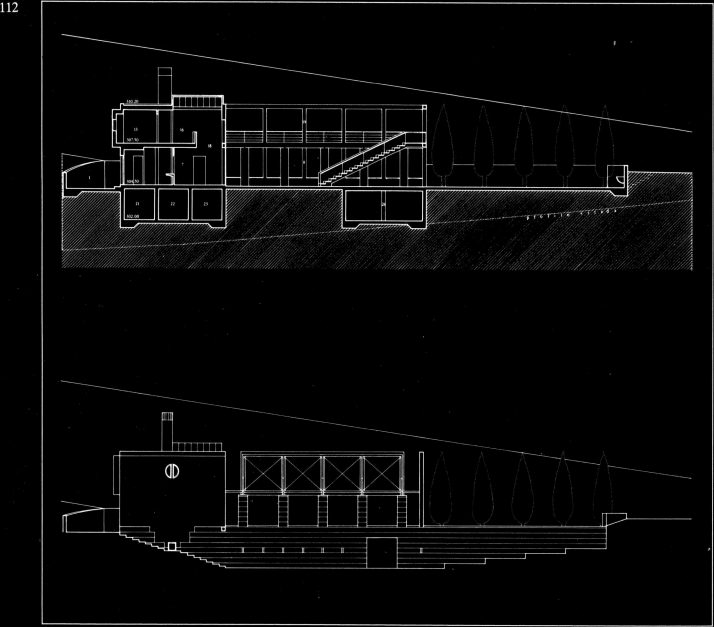

4 Top: section; bottom: west elevation.
5 Cross sections.

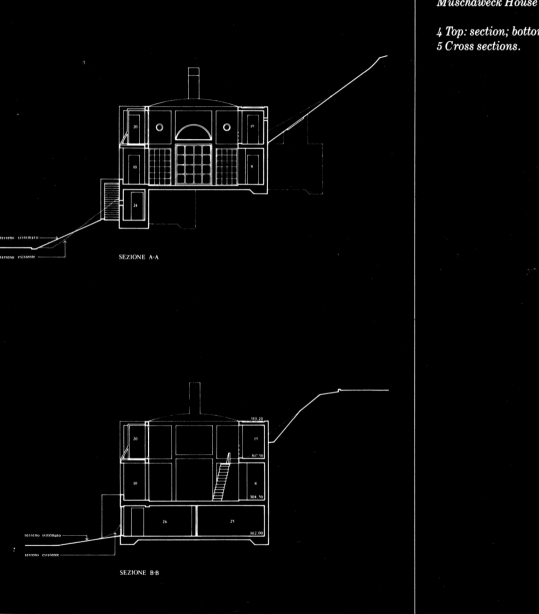

SEZIONE A-A

SEZIONE B-B

ROWHOUSES

Massagno, Switzerland   1985

1

The program for this design stipulated inexpensive housing on a small site. The site lies at the periphery of Lugano, close to a highway intersection, at the edge of a quarter made up largely of villas. The two parcels constituting the site belonged to two different owners and were not really suited for villas; thus they remained undeveloped. The plan to develop middle-income living quarters at the site was in keeping with the fact that it is located not far from the center of the city, thus the necessary infrastructure is nearby. To the south the site overlooks a large old park, and to the north a small urban garden separates the site from the intersection.

The intention was to erect a multi-house urban structure that would stabilize the urban spread and act as a unified architectural entity. The image of a large uniform facade, behind which single houses maintain their individual character, relates to precedents in Paris, London, and Torino (e.g. the Place des Vosges, London Crescent, and Via del Po).

Rather than employ the early modern rowhouse vocabulary of the repetition of a house unit, yielding to a rhythmic building volume, with interior spaces related to exterior spaces, our idea was to attempt to unify the buildings as a whole. This is expressed through axial symmetry and the formulation of frontal elements. Thus, the single house is not emphasized, but is subordinated to the whole. The elements at both ends of this bar articulate the east-west frontage facing the streets.

Within the urban context this bar acts as an ordering and enclosing device. It stabilizes the space at the periphery of the city, and it acts as a boundary. Although the houses are relatively inexpensively built, and not very large, they are generously designed: ceiling heights reach almost nine feet and there are double-height entries, as well as terraces, balconies, and semi-enclosed seating spaces.

115

2

3

116

4

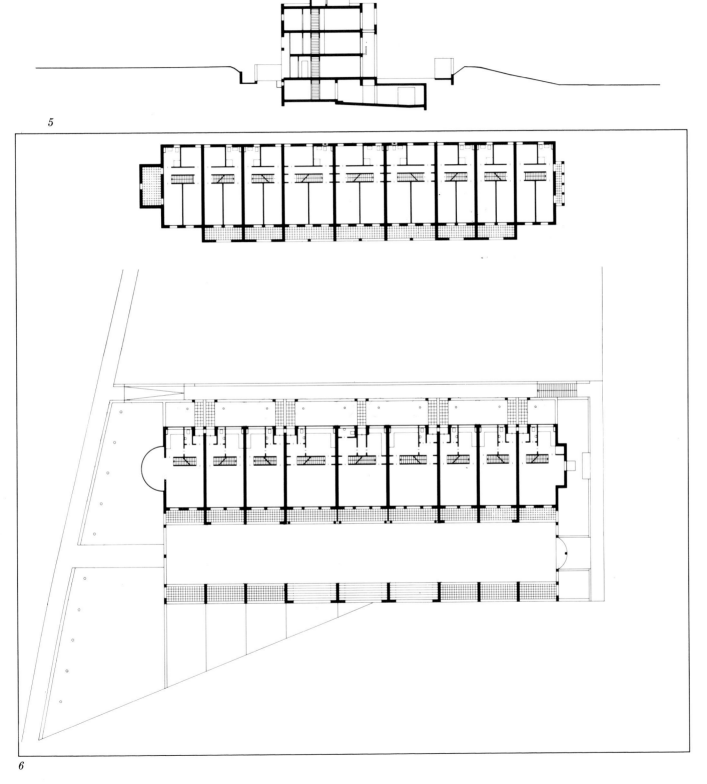

5

6

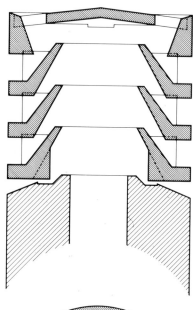

8

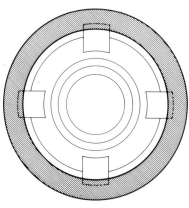

9

7

118

Rowhouses

7 Drawing of chimney details.
8 Garage wall detail.
9 East facade.
10 South facade detail.

10

11, 12 Interior view of an apartment.

120

11

CHURCH IN GIOVA

Giova, Switzerland   1986

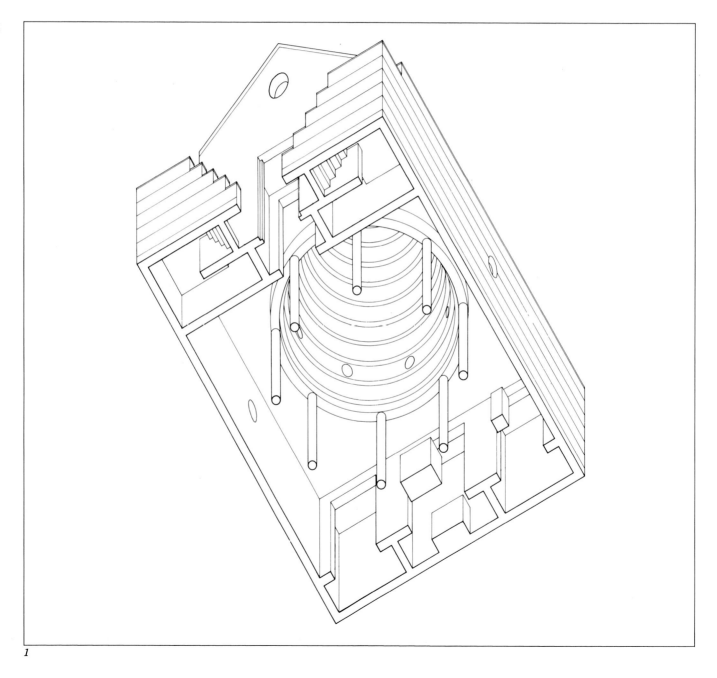

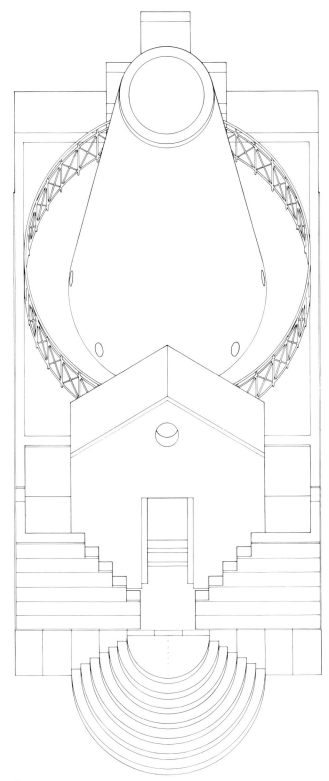

This church should relate . . . to the canons of meditation between God and the world, to "recall" our vocation toward a higher spirit and to a "shining light" that illuminates man's path.
Giornale del Populo, *June 26, 1984*

123

The site for Our Lady of Fatima Church is located in the canton of Grisons, on a slightly declining, hollow plateau that is situated in the center of a mountain range; toward the southwest can be seen the plain of the Magadino. A small, practically flat plot is situated at the edge of the plateau, which ends abruptly in a steep slope at its southern border. The place in which the church is erected is the center of a vast space.

The central plan and the vertical development of the building correspond to the idea of physical centrality in relation to the place from which it rises, symbolizing the universality of the Church. The east facade schematically represents the classic form of the tympanum and refers to the traditional building forms of this region. The central volume, the tower, and the cupola recall the theme of the "shining light." The circular path on the roof allows access to the church, should the interior be closed. The synthesis of, and the analogies proposed by, the references suggest the symbol of the *turris eburnea.*

The church will accommodate fifty to eighty people. Its elevation wall are to be constructed of "ytong" blocks, which are light in weight and insulate effectively. The framework will be of reinforced concrete, with stucco walls inside and out; the base and roof will be surfaced in granite panels.

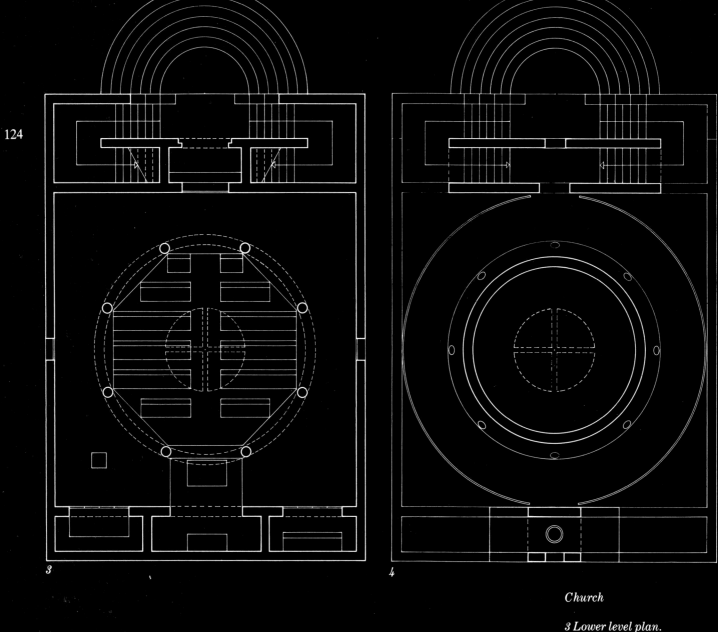

124

Church

3 *Lower level plan.*
4 *Upper level plan.*
5 *Longitudinal section.*

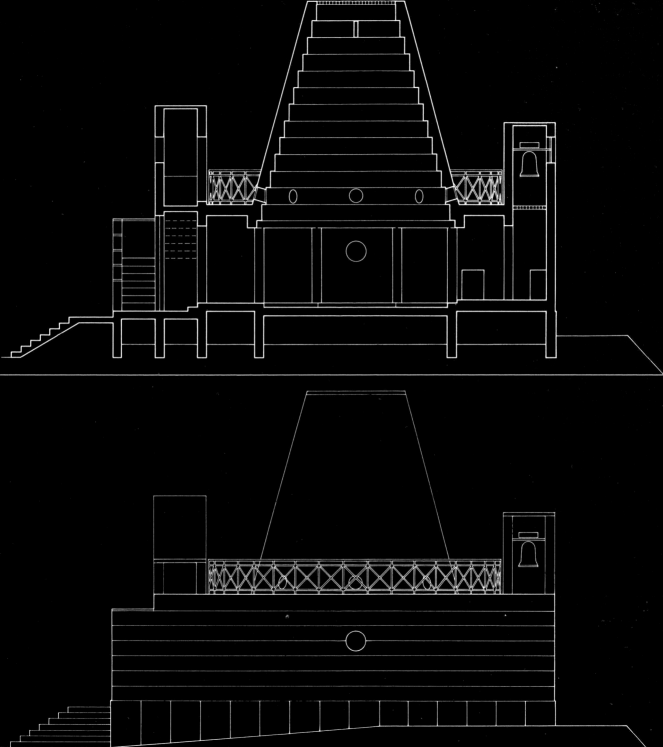

KRESS HOUSE

Massagno, Switzerland   1986

126 The Kress House sits on a very steep site overlooking the magnificent landscape of the Ticino area around Lake Lugano. After the Felder House (1979) this was our second attempt to utilize a courtyard typology. It resulted in a "half-courtyard" house.

The courtyard type reveals itself to be particularly appropriate to very small sites with neighboring houses in close proximity (a common site condition in Switzerland) because it provides spatial and visual privacy. The plan of the house includes a rectangle in which all of the rooms housing the living activities are placed. In addition, two wings define the courtyard space and act, as in the Felder House, as a two-way system that enables an extension of the house towards the courtyard and into nature, while it simultaneously seizes and fixes the presence of the surrounding landscape into the court.

In architectural and stylistic terms, this design represents an effort to reuse the language of the Modern Movement in a critical manner, even while its historical models extend further back into history, to the Roman house and its subsequent transformation as a type.

1 Axonometric.
2 Top left: east elevation; top right: north elevation; middle left: west elevation; middle right: cross section; bottom left: ground floor plan; bottom right: ground floor plan; bottom right: first floor plan.

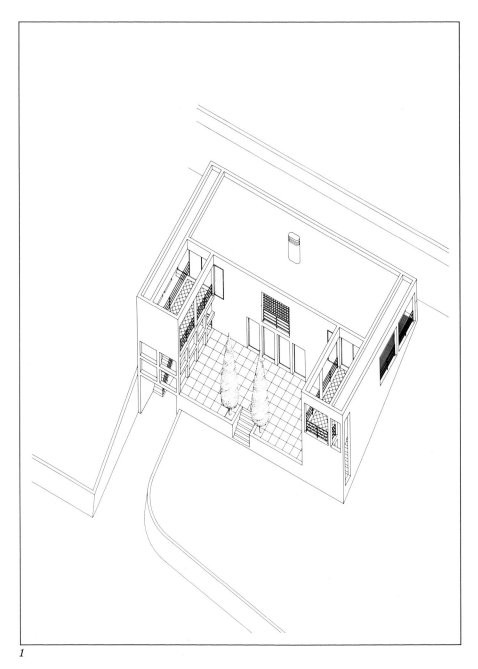

1

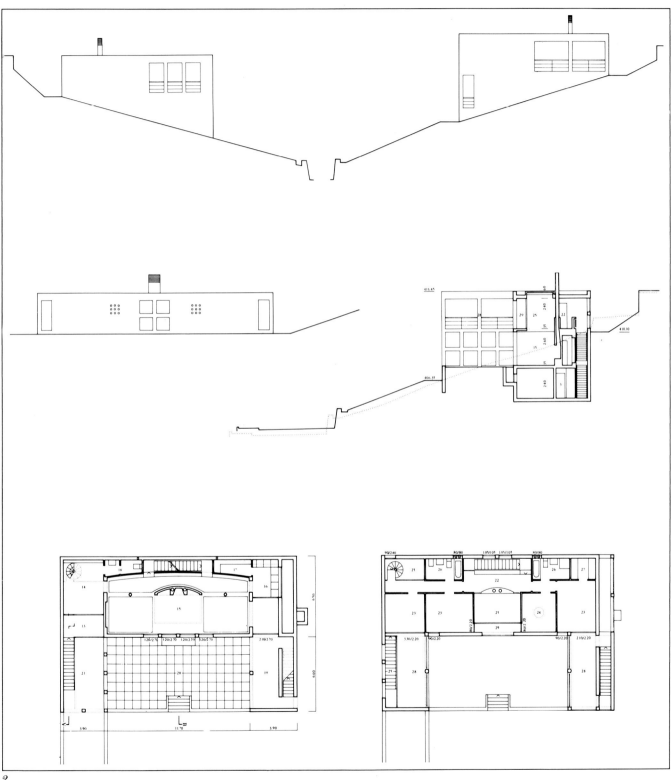